Social Psychology of Musicianship

ROBERT HENLEY WOODY, SR., PhD, ScD, JD

Published by
Meredith Music Publications
a division of G.W. Music, Inc.
1584 Estuary Trail, Delray Beach, Florida 33483
http://www.meredithmusic.com

MEREDITH MUSIC PUBLICATIONS and its stylized double M logo are trademarks of
MEREDITH MUSIC PUBLICATIONS, a division of G.W. Music, Inc.

Cover and text design: Shawn Girsberger

International Standard Book Number: 978-1-57463-198-2
Cataloging-in-Publication Data is on file with the Library of Congress.
Library of Congress Control Number: 2012951719
Printed and bound in U.S.A.

DEDICATION

As an undergraduate music major at Western Michigan University,
the Chair of the Department of Music,
Professor Elwyn Carter, EdD [1913–1998],
became an academic and artistic advisor, teacher, mentor,
career counselor, and "father figure"—this book is dedicated to him
(see Woody, 1999a).

CONTENTS

PREFACE

When anyone asks me to identify myself, I bypass the politically correct response of "I'm a father and husband," and cut to the chase by telling them what I do to earn a living (which is what most new acquaintances are interested in hearing). I say, "I'm a professor, psychologist, and attorney—but I am foremost a musician." In other words, although my first three titles have afforded the greatest career "glory" and income, my self-concept resides with my involvement with music.

This book is about musicianship in its many forms. Although the focus is on information for people who sing or play a musical instrument and want improve their musicianship through effective social relations, others can benefit as well. I consider musicianship to include various levels of involvement; it can encompass simply listening to music or informal singing or playing for oneself alone. But it can go further. It can involve learning (including analysis of the musical elements), practicing, teaching, arranging, composing, or performing for others. By adding social psychology to the mix, many of us can recognize how our connection to music will help and be influenced by relationships with others, whether in nonmusical or musical situations.

Music is an inextricable part of modern life. My basic thesis is two-fold: first, I consider music to be an essential ingredient for healthy psychological development; and second, everyone needs to nurture his or her musical potential in order to gain self-enrichment, which can lead to better social relationships. Said bluntly, everyone can be a stakeholder in musicianship. I refer to this psychological principle as "generalized musicianship."

What I just said should not be misconstrued. In the realm of generalized musicianship, not everyone aspires nor is able to become a professional entertainer. By my definition, the person does not need to perform in front of others, but there should be an effort to benefit psychologically from the world of music.

Back in the 1950s, Meredith Willson's classic "The Music Man" told the world how every child had musical potential and that capitalizing on it would change the community. In 1995, the film "Mr. Holland's Opus," depicted how a school music teacher is not always appreciated in the social hierarchy of a school faculty, but impacts students in a way that inspires them to have meaningful lives and treasure their musical experiences forever. These movies reflect the social psychology of music.

The contents of this book are geared primarily to musicians, from the raw beginner to the Super Star. The information is applicable to all vocalists and instrumentalists, regardless of musical genre. In addition to the psychological contributions made to the musician and his or her social contacts, the information will accelerate and enrich actual musicianship.

Much of what I present will be about how being musical is facilitated by social relationships, and vice versa. That is, the major purpose of this book is to help the reader understand how thoughts, communications, and contacts between people can influence and be influenced by music. There is reciprocity of influence between music and social relations.

In order to avoid burdensome scholarly citations, whenever I say "research supports" to preface a principle from social psychology, the point is so well-established that turning to almost any undergraduate textbook suitable for a social psychology class will provide the research sources for the point of view.

If there is ever a term used that needs a definition or I provide a definition that seems questionable, a good source for confirmation of the information is: VandenBos, G. R. (2007). *APA dictionary of psychology.* Washington, DC: American Psychological Association.

Also, everyone knows that there are many (countless?) types of music that could justly be referred to as a genre (a distinctive category). Since it is impractical to repeatedly provide a laundry list of genres, I will generally refer to classical, jazz, rock, popular, and country, knowing that each term is an umbrella for many other specific types of music.

Incidentally, any attempt to pigeonhole my musical interests is doomed for failure. With most of my musical mentors, I had the good fortune of being guided into realizing that music is music, regardless of genre. That is, a music teacher or professor, who might be expected to press me into "high-falutin" classical music, seldom urged me to reject other types of music. In fact, most of my musical mentors encouraged exploring every genre possible.

I am delighted that, to this day, I am interested in and sing or play music from several genres. Since I know music theory, I am able to learn, read, analyze, practice, transpose, arrange, compose, and improvise music, all of which enable me to avoid genre-related barriers.

Not to be insulting, any musician who is restricted to a single genre, no matter how skilled or talented, is missing out by not being in full-bodied musicianship. Part of my master plan is to encourage every reader to cross genre lines and pursue full-bodied musicianship.

The proof of this point is obvious. Notice how certain celebrity entertainers "indulge" in various genres (e.g., Itzak Perlman, Yo Yo Ma, Wynton Marsalis, Edgar Meyer, and the list goes on and on). One night in a Nashville haven for country music, I sat next to one of the aforementioned classical musicians; he had played the night before with the local symphony, but all evening long, was attentive to and avidly photographed the country musicians. Also, in Nashville, it is common for the "sidemen," male or female, to the country music celebrities to play classical, jazz, rock, and popular music in other venues.

As might be assumed, I drew from my advanced academic training in nonmusical areas (education, psychology, health, and law) to analyze the social psychology of music. Likewise, my decades of work as a musician gave me insight about human behavior. While working on this book, I had flashbacks of almost every music educator or performer with whom I have had contact, from my first Hawaiian guitar teacher, to my university mentors, to symphony musicians who shaped my abilities, to my fellow musicians in smoke-filled bars, concert halls, and television, radio, and recording studios.

Among my actual musical experiences, I gained insights from the opportunities for possible musical celebrity that I turned down in order to pursue the security that comes from higher education. Thankfully, I do not bemoan any of the dismissed opportunities to be, as the movie character Bull Durham (Kevin Costner) said, "up in the 'show'." I will share what I have learned about making logical and prudent judgments about musical choices and behaviors, recognizing that what worked for me may require adaptation by others.

My hope and intent is to help the reader, whether a nonmusician or a musician, gain an understanding of how music provides personal benefits that derive from social relations and how social relations, in turn, influence musicianship. The outcome that I promote is for everyone to experience musical enrichment.

Robert Henley Woody, Sr.
Omaha, NE

ACKNOWLEDGMENTS

Countless family members, friends, and musical colleagues, teachers, and performers have shaped my musicianship. I extend appreciation to each of them.

A special note of appreciation is given to my son, Robert H. Woody, III, now a professor of music at the University of Nebraska-Lincoln, who taught me a great deal about the psychology of music; however, he is certainly not to be faulted for any of my shortcomings.

1
Musical Overture

When humming or singing in the shower or the car or being alone and trying to sing or play an instrument, there is musicianship. To lay claim on being a musician, there should, however, be two things: a *conscious commitment* to the singing or playing; and a *motivation to improve* the self-determined quality. As I will explain, the potential payoffs are great.

To become a musician, neither formal lessons (from a teacher) nor self-directed study (reading books) is mandatory—but these sources of learning are usually helpful. This "vernacular music making" (informally learning through trial-and-error and explorations) principle (Cohen, 2006) has adaptive application to other musical genres as well.

Developing musical potential requires consideration of one's life and identification of a starting point for becoming a musician. This book will help that self-examination and effort. For example, throughout the book, I will tell you about my personal experiences, such as how I became interested in music, what I tried to do musically, and the frustrations and benefits that I experienced. This sharing of my life experiences is intended to model how one goes about doing a self-analysis of musicianship. Further, all of the situations that I describe capture the "social relations" that were present, in other words, how people influenced the music and, in turn, how music influenced the people.

Musical Awareness and Appreciation

The first step towards musicianship is to listen to and be aware of music. Aside from appreciating the sounds of nature, there may well be other benefits from being still and silent and listening to the world around you. Some of the sounds heard, like those made by passing traffic or neighbor children playing, do not constitute music.

Are the sounds of nature, say the chirping by birds, considered to be music? Maybe. Scholars continue to debate this question. Since the common definition for music is that it is controlled sound, which means that there is a pattern of sounds with different pitches that communicate for a useful purpose, primitive sounds for the *joie de vivre* are present with birds, but probably do not contribute to the origins of human musicianship (Storr, 1992).

To be aware of music, a formal analysis of the musical elements is not always necessary. It is enough to do the auditory processing of the musical sounds, and hopefully be open to some sort of experiential change, physical or psychological, because of having heard the music.

For example, as will be discussed throughout this book, music triggers emotional responses. To become aware of music, you should let your inclinations lead to emotions and recognize them as positive or negative (just use everyday language, like a song "makes me happy" or "depressed" or whatever). This will further your music appreciation. Storr (1992) joins me, with the comment: "even listeners who cannot read musical notation and who have never attempted to learn an instrument may be so deeply affected that, for them, any day which passes without being seriously involved with music in one way or another is a day wasted" (p. x).

Also in the vein of appreciation, anyone—including those without any formal training in music—can start to discern sounds that seem pleasurable and are preferred, as opposed to the opposite. Logically, the listener to music develops preferences and appreciates different aspects or types of music. I will say more later about why each of us has particular music preferences, but for now it is enough to acknowledge that deciding consciously to like or dislike a musical performance or genre opens the door to musicianship.

Personal appreciation of the music is "instrumental" (serves a purpose). The listener to or performer of music must contemplate the sounds and then project his or her self-characteristics into it, thus creating an empathic identification.

There is also aesthetic appreciation, relevant to the structure and substance (i.e., form and order) of the music. Both empathy and aesthetics are linked to extraversion and introversion, and people differ in their emotional involvement versus intellectual (emotionally detached) approach (Worringer, 1963).

When I try to draw people into singing along with me, I often encounter someone who says, "I can't sing." My response, without being too serious, is, "You mean that you have never tried to sing." Then with a touch of humor, I get them to join with me, even if it is speaking the words as an echo of something that I have just sung. Soon the novice singer is varying pitches. As time passes, I persistently keep drawing the person into singing. I have had countless people who once claimed, "I can't sing," end up singing with gusto.

It is not the quality of the musical performance as heard by other people that determines one's musicianship, it is just the performance itself. Just doing it is the solution to entering into the world of music. To lay claim on musicianship, only the person needs to determine whether his or her performance is acceptable (for the moment) or not.

The foregoing information about awareness and appreciation also contributes to a definition of music. Varying the tonal elements organizes the sounds, which then becomes a purposeful act—which is part of music performance.

Music in Life

Many treatises on music are quick to claim that there has never been a culture that did not have some form of music (Levitin, 2006). Often the sounds of nature or daily living are cited as the source of human (and animal?) interest in musical sounds.

From the scientific perspective, Ball (2010) cynically says, "And about the origins of music, we have almost no evidence whatsoever" (p.18). Working daily with university students, I suspect that the modern-day student of music would probably join the chorus, saying something like, "What difference does it make to know about the creation of music in prehistoric times, I want to know about music in my lifetime?"

Pragmatics rule out, but it is worth recognizing that there is no contradiction to the idea that music, by some definition, has always been present in societies. This concept adds to the importance of considering music to be an essential part of life.

Social Behavior and Music

To explain social behavior, evolutionary psychology relies on genetic factors that have evolved over time (relevant to natural selection and survival). In other words, it is often said that ancient music lessened risks by soothing emotions of potential enemies. Another evolutionary idea that should be a bit provocative, even to today's hard-to-convince university students, is that music has an underlying sexual component. Yes, Sigmund Freud [1856–1939] would be proud (and more will be said later about Freudian ideas). It was, however, Charles Darwin [1808–1882] (2004) who thought that music did not have an adaptive function, music was particularly for sexual selection. That is, music could be used to promote a reproductive advantage, which had the appeal of continuing one's self.

Given that musical performances are intended to please and be enjoyed by others (such as an audience), it is easy to see that a person exhibiting musical talent could be attractive to potential sexual partners. Also, musical ability may be a predictor of male reproductive prowess (for example, by increasing testosterone) (Ball, 2010). Sluming and Manning (2000) add tantalizing data, documenting that, at classical concerts with predominantly male musicians, females in the audience tend to sit nearer the orchestras.

At popular music concerts, this same conduct occurs. For example, although seating was arranged no doubt, the stage in the iconic "Elvis: '68 Comeback" (DVD, Presley Enterprises, 2006) is surrounded for several rows of almost exclusively females, some startlingly young and nubile (this may also be depicting the alleged lifelong attraction that Elvis Presley [1935–1977] had for young teenagers (Nash, 2010).

Likewise, from the advent of Beatle Mania, there has been a continuing inclination at rock concerts for females to throw undergarments to the musicians on the stage. The same does not, of course, occur in reverse. Has a male audience member ever thrown an undergarment at a female performer? I doubt it.

Having a Ball

In *The Music Instinct* (2010), Philip Ball [1962–] places perceptual psychology and neurological factors at the forefront: "We are pattern seekers, clue-solvers, unravellers of sensory data, and also communicators and story-tellers" (p. 409). Given his PhD in physics from Bristol University (and long-time Editor of *Nature*), it is not surprising that Ball views music scientifically.

Ball believes that music is a constructive force for intellect and for the body and culture. However, he does not neglect the social context, recognizing that musical cognition does not occur in a value-free vacuum. In fact, he goes so far as to say, "There's a good argument that music is better defined in sociological and cultural than in acoustic terms" (p. 10), and adds, "Ethnomusicologists have documented an abundance of social functions for music: it expresses emotions, induces pleasure, accompanies dance, validates rituals and institutions, promotes social stability" (p. 11). Sociologically, music is so powerful, it can bring about social harmony or discord. In the process, it shapes the character of the people.

After noting the Darwinian sexual selection hypothesis, Ball elevates the importance of social psychology: "One of the most obvious features of music the world over is that it tends to be a group activity. Even when performed by a select few, music commonly happens in places and contexts in which it creates social cohesion, for example in religion and ritual or in dance and communal singing" (p. 25).

Ball seems to make the individual impact of music secondary to the benefits from music that provides advantages to an entire society or culture. Said differently, he believes that music can produce a lasting sense of togetherness. Individual effects may promote sexual self-control, lower aggression, and other socializing functions.

What's in Storr?

Anthony Storr [1920–2001] was a distinguished British psychiatrist, with a psychoanalytic orientation. He was a prolific author, mainly of books interpreting Freudian theory, especially theoretical ideas from Sigmund Freud and Carl Jung [1875–1961]. In addition to *The Dynamics of Creation* (1993), his analysis of music is epitomized by *Music and the Mind* (1992).

Unlike popular misconception, Storr did not attach neurosis to creativity, but viewed it as a nourishing and integrative impulse, capable of being linked to a desire for power, wealth, prestige, or sexual conquest. He ended *Music and the Mind* with an acknowledgement of how music had incomparably enriched his life: "It is an irreplaceable, underserved, transcendental blessing" (p. 188).

Since psychoanalytic writings are commonly suspect for subjectivity, Storr's profound personalized conclusion may well merit concern for the objectivity of his work. Although he was not a scientific (empirical) researcher, he was seemingly a sensitive and intellectually keen integrationist of the scholarly work of others.

Storr supported that everyone by nature possesses the physiological and cognitive processes used to produce music. If this is true, almost every person has the potential to produce music—which is one of my principal points.

Accordingly, Storr believed that the human brain is programmed to respond to emotional and intonational aspects of the human voice (for example, infants responding to rhythm, pitch, intensity, and timbre of the caregiver's voice), and this progresses to responding to music with emotional and physiological arousal within the neurological system. Certainly emotion is always a filter: "we recognize that some composers habitually select certain keys when they want to express particular emotions" (Storr, 1992, p. 43). Storr found it is interesting that the sound that is sung tends to be louder than a spoken word, suggesting the power of music is aided by volume. He also recognized that musical material tends to be remembered longer than material that is simply read.

In neo-Freudian fashion, Storr acknowledged that social relationships influence the individual, which would surely have met with the wrath of Sigmund Freud (Benjamin, 2007). He noted that some ensemble religious music is "more concerned with enhancing group feeling . . . than with promoting the individual's relation with God" (p. 22); and he added: "As the capacity for speech and conceptual thought developed, music became less important as a way of conveying information, but retained its significance as a way of communicating feelings and cementing bonds between individuals, especially in group situations" (p. 23). The principle of promoting group over individual identification is, of course, common to all varieties of music.

The Musical Brain

Anyone who has studied music knows that the intense focus that is required involves cognitive processing similar to solving mathematical problems. Having just acquired a ten-string steel guitar with multiple foot and knee pedals, one fellow told me, "In learning to play the monster, my brain has never been so taxed, it's like computing statistical formulas."

As for the neurological component of musicianship, research supports a broad potential for musical ability: "Virtually all children are born with the full neural capacities to engage with music," which is "stimulated and developed by musical activities in the home environment" (Lehmann, Sloboda, & Woody, 2007, p. 41). Moreover, the "level of achievement seems to be directly related to the level of opportunity freely available within the society" (p. 40). These researchers conclude that, "we can already be fairly certain that at least 96% of the general population has the innate capacity to deal with music" (p. 30).

Since everyone has his or her own neurological structure, the interaction between music and brain is always idiosyncratic. Levitin (2006) says: "Like science, music over the years has proved to be an adventure, never experienced exactly the same way twice" (p. 11), and he believes that music has the potential to further understanding of "our motives, fears, desires, memories, and even communication in the broadest sense" (p. 12)—each of these functions has, of course, neurological bases.

Music has a powerful influence on the human brain. Some people with neurological damage can achieve movement with music that could not be achieved otherwise. Seizures can be induced by music, such as by, say (for some people), a vacillation of high-pitched sounds that creates neurological driving.

Music is primarily processed in the right hemisphere of the brain, with the left hemisphere of the brain being for language. The difference between the contributions to music made by the dual hemispheres is an issue of logic and emotion, not words versus music per se (Storr, 1992).

For example, much ado has been made about Mel Tillis, a primary stutterer, being able to articulate flawlessly while singing, but stammering when speaking the same words. This difference is probably due to the left hemisphere encoding the pattern that is stammered, with the right hemisphere processing the sounds that are sung.

It is a popular notion that music can change a person's neurological system. For example, numerous studies support that engaging in music influences neural circuitry in nonmusical areas of the brain (Rauscher, 1997; Rauscher, Shaw, Levine, Wright, Dennis, & Newcomb, 1997). In a search for improved neural functioning, this notion explains why parents play music to infants and music therapists get Alzheimer's patients involved in musical activities.

Although neuroscience can, figuratively and literally, dissect music processes with cold objectivity, more research on these real-life strategies is needed. That said, to date, the research seems clear that there are reciprocal influences between music and the brain, but obviously there are other influences on one's neurology (particularly, I believe, from social reinforcements). A later discussion of nature (hereditary or constitutional-genetic) versus nurture (environmental or experiential) will delve further into the neurological aspects of music.

Music and Society

Given that there is an integral reciprocity of influences between music and groups of people, it is logical that the structure of a society could be influenced as well. Sloboda (1985) accepts that music is an organizational tool for society: "Music, perhaps, provides a unique mnemonic framework within which humans can express, by the temporal organization of sound and gesture, the structure of their knowledge of and social relations" (p. 267). Blacking (1987) states: "Through musical interaction, two people create forms that are greater than the sum of the parts, and make for themselves experiences of empathy that would be unlikely to occur in ordinary social intercourse" (p. 26). Uniting with Sloboda and Blacking, Storr (1992) said: "Music has the effect of intensifying or underlining the emotion which a particular event calls forth, by simultaneously coordinating the emotions of a group of people" (p. 24).

The mode, style, or genre of music being heard or performed by a group casts a firm framework around social functions. Blacking (1987) offers, "Human attitudes and specifically human ways of thinking about the world are the results of dance and song" (p. 60). Extending the human ways of thinking to a society, Greek philosophers Plato and Socrates opined that music was essential to production within a society and that changes in the "modes of music" led to the fundamental laws of the state (government) changing (Dodds, 1951).

Music can heighten the emotions at a political rally, with a subsequent impact on the society. As reflected in Hitler's era, music was used to marshal Germany for war. In a peaceful vein, consider how performers like Toby Keith, Lee Greenwood, Kate Smith, Pete Seeger, Odetta, Paul Robeson, Woody and Arlo Guthrie, John Denver, and Peter, Paul, and Mary—and the list goes on and on—rally fervor for a particular political or social cause through use of music. Blacking (1987) offers an optimistic proclamation that: "music can become a universal language when individuals are acquainted with all forms of artistic musical expression, and through the transformation of individuals it becomes a [citing Percy Grainger] 'vehicle for world peace and the unification of mankind'" (p. 149).

At this juncture, it is sufficient to acknowledge that music has a deep-seated connection to the human psyche, whether within an individual, between two people, or inherent to a society. Military bands have certainly produced greater patriotism. Choirs have induced mass audiences to mourn (such as during the funeral for a national leader). And perhaps most obvious, the "flapper" era contributed to views about prohibition at the macro level, while rock 'n roll created a new generation of musical aficionados. The Woodstock Nation was born in a single festival.

A powerful musical presence can impact a community. Growing up in Kalamazoo, Michigan, I was aware of the Gibson Guitar Company. Since Orville Gibson sold his first instruments in 1894 and established the Gibson Mandolin-Guitar Manufacturing Company in 1902, the Gibson Company's influence on the community was far more than employing some of its residents.

As its reputation for building fine fretted instruments ascended, so did the Gibson's integration into the Kalamazoo culture. The city increasingly sensed, especially perhaps after the profound role guitars assumed in popular music during the 1950s, a cultural pride from having the Gibson Company there.

When Gibson closed its Kalamazoo operations in 1984, it was like a cloud had descended on the musical mecca. There was denial, such as trying to cling to the past by the founding of the Heritage Guitar Company, composed of some of the Gibson Company equipment and a few of its former employees.

For those of us with sensitivity to the community's cultural spirit, it was clear that closing Gibson's operations in Kalamazoo had a negative impact. Similarly, the 1995 merger between Upjohn and Pharmacia AB of Sweden and the subsequent closing of the famous Upjohn Pharmaceutical Company further dampened the community's pride in having a unique industrial identity.

Similar community spirit has resulted from a musical reputation linked to a place. As but a few examples, consider: symphonies and opera companies in Boston, Chicago, and Philadelphia (and many other places); Motown in Detroit; the jazz and folk scene in Chicago, Boston, and New York; the Mormon Tabernacle Choir in Salt Lake; the blues and "jass" produced in New Orleans, Chicago, and Memphis, along with rockabilly from the latter; the country music of Austin, Bakersfield, Branson, and Nashville; the Rock and Roll Hall of Fame in Cleveland; and of course the recording scene in Los Angeles, Minneapolis, Nashville, and New York. The list could go on and on.

In turn, the community's musical spirit bathes the people who live there. I have no doubt that my growing up in Kalamazoo during the heyday of the Gibson Guitar Company and being mentored by two of its executives, Julius Bellson (Woody, 1978a & b) and Wilbur Marker (Woody, 1981), provided a strong incentive for me to pursue music, especially fretted instruments.

The *coup d' grace* may be that public school music programs enhance the appreciation of music and learning for the total culture. Bloom (1987) considers music to be highly educative, and cautions that allowing any one musical genre (say rock 'n roll) to dominate for a long period of time could potentially "close the mind" to new learning and ideas.

2

Music Psychology

From music, the person's mind, body, and spirit gain nourishment. The sustenance and fortification come from loudness (amplitude or volume), pitch (the relative position of a tone in a musical scale), contour (the structural shape of a melody or musical line of notes), rhythm (a series of durations for a sequence of sounds at different pitches), tempo (the speed or pace), timbre (tonal color), spatial location (grouping of sounds from the same relative position), and reverberation (perception of distance). All of the foregoing principles, factors, or musical elements are subject to the neurological organization of the attributes or dimensions of meter (rhythm and loudness cues), harmony (hierarchy between tones), and melody (the main theme, influenced by the musical genre). Elaboration of these concepts or factors may be found in Levitin (2006). The human brain is capable of distinguishing and separating these attributes.

Vibrations are the triggers for sounds. Objects can vibrate (some more than others); the result creates the potential for the proverbial sound in the forest that must be processed by the auditory component of the brain to be deemed to "exist."

Instrumental Sonics

Any musical sound is more than the fundamental tone; there are overtones (other frequencies) sounding as well. Each musical instrument has a unique overtone profile. For example, a trumpet has a different overtone profile than, say, a violin. Indeed, if you have two of the same instrument, say two cellos, one will actually be different than the other.

On several occasions when I have been purchasing an instrument, I arranged to go to the factory or warehouse to try out several instruments in order to choose the one with the sonic (sound waves produced) qualities that seemed most pleasing to me. Granted, it is a subjective decision. As I tried several instruments with the same brand and of the same model, I would find that the sound was a bit different.

Often there is no one sound that is required or "best." Every person responds to different factors. For example, among my mandolins, I tend to prefer a certain style (A-model) for classical and jazz music and another style (F-model) for popular and country music. Of course, there are differences between, say, the several A-models, and the same is true for the F-models. Shortly I will say more about this idea when applied to choice of guitars.

When choosing an instrument, brand and reputation of a model do not assure quality. For example, I own two collector-quality Gibson tenor banjos (a Florentine from the late 1920s and a 1976 All-American); because of their ornate carvings and gold trim, both have been displayed in museums. However, I also own a tenor Kennedy banjo, which fewer people know about.

It turns out that, back in the 1960s, a Gibson luthier and banjo technician, Davis Kennedy, had a way to alter the banjo rim itself (the tone ring) and he later made so-called Kennedy banjos. Reportedly Earl Scruggs used a Kennedy banjo on the iconic recording of "Foggy Mountain Breakdown" (http://www.banjowizard.com/tonebell.htm). With my aforementioned three banjos, everyone who has heard them has agreed that the sound of the relatively unknown brand and model (the Kennedy) produces a far superior sound when compared to the other much more valuable Gibson collectibles.

With guitars, there is a comparable principle. Whether the musical genre is classical, jazz, rock, popular, ethnic, folk, or country music, the guitar is the sentinel for rhythm and often a solo voice as well. When it comes to determining an accompaniment by guitar, I believe that the "musical style" of the piece is foremost consideration. That is, the melody, harmony, and genre are not necessarily the primary determinants of what accompaniment the guitarist should play (Woody, 2010).

Among other things, the size of the ensemble and the "musical message" merit consideration. Also, the issue of whether other instruments will be playing is highly important for the selection process.

Of relevance to the discussion about differences in sonics and using acoustic guitar as a point of reference, I believe that: finger picking (alternating bare fingers or sometimes using finger picks) is best for semi- and classical music; parlor style (bass-strum) is suitable for soloist or small ensemble music; swing style (comping) does well with jazz; and concert style (block chords) creates a snare drum effect, useful in popular and country music. Add these considerations to whether the instrument is an archtop or flattop, and there will be quiet a palette of sonic colors from which the musician can choose. Each of these options has an impact on the sound.

As mentioned earlier, even among instruments of the same type, sonic differences will exist. Beyond finger picking for classical music played on nylon strings, I use a flattop guitar with steel strings to accompany voices, but rely on an archtop with steel strings for larger (louder) ensemble work, regardless of genre. As with the mandolins that I described, I might use Archtop #1 for one song and Archtop #2 for another song, with the choice determined by the sound that I want to produce. Of course, another point is the totally different sounds from acoustic versus electrified guitars.

There are, of course, various materials to construct a particular instrument. A clarinetist with whom I perform has a fine collection of woodwind instruments. Just after he added a new Eb clarinet made of a rare and impressively grained Brazilian wood, we discussed the array of instruments that he owned. He was able to articulate the sound differences that he achieved, as attributed to the materials used to make a given clarinet.

Regarding an instrument's sound, some musicians believe that an instrument will change if it is played frequently versus remaining idle, kept out of its case, or if a virtuoso plays it. As Palmer (2006) states: "Fine instruments must be played. This is true for violins, banjos, guitars—all instruments. There are groups who tour with the Stradivarius violins that are in several museums, just to make sure they maintain their ability to vibrate properly" (unnumbered). Supposedly this concept applies to all sorts of instruments—the principle being that producing sounds on a music instrument changes its physical properties.

For example, when I was playing in the "Nashville Scene," I encountered a number of bluegrass mandolinists who believed that the "breaking in" of any new mandolin required positioning it in front of stereo speakers for forty hours while CD recordings by Bill Monroe played night and day. When no mandolinist endorsed more or less than forty hours, I decided that an urban myth was present! All of the musicians telling me about this practice were confident, however, that this passive exposure produced positive results, believing that it was due to the physical properties of the instrument changing (adopting the sonics that Bill Monroe's instrument produced). None wanted to consider that it might be a change in perception due to the bluegrass culture endorsing and creating the expectancy (the power of suggestion preordained the perceptual outcome?). Incidentally, this same process has been described for impacting a guitar (http://www.banjowizard.com/tonebell.htm).

Anyone who has taken an introductory psychology course has heard about "magical thinking," which is "the belief that events or the behavior of others can be influenced by one's thoughts, wishes, or rituals" (VandenBos, 2007, p. 548). Although this is common among young children, one would hope that no adult would hold that sort of view. However, the iconic Hawaiian guitarist Jerry Byrd [1920–2005] goes a step further. In his autobiography, he tells about a custom-made pedal steel guitar that he thought was awful and, in disgust, finally shouted at the instrument as he put it away, "When I come here tomorrow, you'd better get with me or . . . [you are] going into the Cumberland River on my way home" (Byrd, 2003, p. 81)! The next day, he asserts, "it had changed completely. It had surrendered" (p. 82)! To which I would have said respectfully to the late Mr. Byrd, "Do you know the meaning of incredulous?"

Nature versus Nurture

People who believe that they are incapable of participating in music often justify it with, "I just have no musical talent." I believe that everyone potentially has musical talent to some degree, but it depends on his or her commitments, opportunities, and social reinforcements. Certain constitutional or genetic components will, however, place a limitation on overall potentials. I will say more about this issue shortly.

A basic question about talent of any kind is whether it is due to nature (hereditary or constitutional-genetic) or nurture (environmental or experiential) or both. According to VandenBos (2007): "Nativists emphasize the role of heredity, whereas environmentalists emphasize social cultural and ecological factors, including family attitudes, child-rearing practices, and economic status. Most scientists now accept that there is a close interaction between hereditary and environmental factors in the ontogeny [development] of behavior" (p. 611).

Talent refers to "an innate skill or ability, or an aptitude to excel in one or more specific activities or subject areas" (p. 921). However, "Talent cannot be accounted for by normal development patterns and is often not maximized, as it requires time, energy, sacrifice, dedication, and money on the part of parents, mentors, and the talented person" (pp. 921–922). As will be discussed, the foregoing definition is clearly applicable to the talents that are relevant to musicianship. From my study of the subject, I am of the mind that musical talent represents a combination of nature and nurture.

As a psychology professor, I find musical talent to be fascinating. In some ways, it defies behavioral science. That is, just when empirical data have been collected, as would define the source and development of musical abilities, new research or a different method for teaching music will uncover previously unrecognized or unmeasured performance factors. The next step is to amass evidence pertaining to what are the causative variables and why these additional considerations were missed (since the latter might reveal flaws in earlier research).

In the past, theories of intelligence have sometimes tried to include musical talent. If there is not a musical mental ability, perhaps it should be included in a broader "artistic" factor or, more likely, in "general" intelligence, referred to as the "g-factor."

Recognizing the limits of the g-factor as an explanation for giftedness, Kirnarskaya (2009) notes: "Psychologists are unable to determine with any degree of certainty exactly which qualities are necessary to master material in some area to the level of known achievement, and which qualities propel us beyond, to the broadening, lengthening, and extension of the previously attained" (p. 7). The foregoing is compatible with: "Given the laborious nature of acquiring musical skills, even for those blessed with the proverbial 'God-given' musical career, it is obvious that extraordinary psychological characteristics are necessary" (Woody, 1999b, p. 241). In practical terms, the research to date supports that endowments by nurture will contribute to musical ability, and the musical self-concept (which embraces psychological factors and motivations) may well provide the cornerstone. This idea is a primary dimension of this book.

When trying to establish a model for talent, Kirnarskaya (2009), relying heavily on the research by Simonton (1999, 2000), endorses an emotional or motivational component: "It has been noted that the desire to give oneself over completely to one's chosen undertaking—understood as an absolutely selfless feeling, unconnected with a striving for glory or personal enrichment—is proportionate to the creative component of one's talent" (p. 15). For those interested in developing musical talent, her views contain two optimistic ingredients. First, professional training seems to distinguish musicians from non-musicians (such as in aural capacities) and second, "much evidence, especially in the neurosciences, speaks in favor of special brain mechanisms responsible for music processing which doesn't exclude certain overlap with other functions" (p. 25). In practical terms, this means that people do differ in endowments by nature, as relevant to developing their musical ability; and although social learning and the musical self-concept are important, biological factors are also influential.

As might be expected, Kirnarskaya's stance is linked to the multiple intelligence theory advocated by Howard Gardner [1943–]. His theory of multiple intelligence posits a wide variety of cognitive abilities. Among those, Gardner identifies musical intelligence, which deals with sensitivity to sounds, rhythms, pitches, meters, tones, melodies, and other facets of music (Gardner, 1993, 1997).

The Gardner theory supports that people with high musical intelligence tend to have good pitch. For example, they do well at singing a note at the right number vibrations per second or putting a finger at the right place on a fretless string instrument. Consequently, these people will be able to sing, play an instrument, and compose better than those with lower musical intelligence.

Beyond this perspective, and this is important, while a relatively low musical intelligence will not accommodate prodigy or giftedness for music, it does not preclude the person from achieving musically in a satisfying way, albeit at a more commonplace level. Incidentally, it is important to recognize that Gardner's ideas have been criticized strongly for being more opinion than scholarship based on data (Sternberg, 1983; Traub, 1995).

Given all of the foregoing, Kirnarskaya (2009) offers six conclusions: general ability does not exist; abilities facilitate assimilation and training (not discovery and invention); talent is multiplicative (operational, creative, and emotional); talent is hereditary in nature; heredity may extend to distant ancestors and indirect relatives; and "abilities, giftedness, and talent become evident and can be assessed only under conditions and using materials which are maximally matched to the specific activities which make up their functional profiles" (p. 35). She places musical talent into a context of cognitive psychology of music and musical neuropsychology, saying: "The data of these sciences on the processes of musical perception and thinking, and on the work of the musical memory and the musical imagination, will become the basis for our model of musical talent" (p. 43). With meticulous writing clarity, Kirnarskaya leaves no key area of research unconsidered (for example, music and mathematics, unity of music and speech). With minimal comment, Kirnarskaya acknowledges social communication: "Music and speech bring about intellectual and emotional exchange between humans, employing the venue of sound toward the end of mutual understanding" (p. 360).

Neuropsychology and cognitive psychology are linked to the nature viewpoint, and are certainly important to talent—but there is more to the story. Research supports that musical ability develops, in part, from social reinforcement, including (but certainly not limited to) the culture in which the person lives and the resources available: "the child from the favored background, both socioeconomically and musically, is thus more likely to develop high levels of musical ability" (Sergent & Thatcher, 1974, p. 55).

Sociocultural Influences

At this point, we find the possible answer for the question of why does one person, and not another, becomes a musician? There is supportive research for believing that "an enriched sociocultural background can facilitate an interest in music" (Woody, 1999b, p. 243). Logically, the importance of neuropsychology and cognitive psychology should also be acknowledged. However, nature is not necessarily determinative of musical outcome, and there should be no denial that sociocultural factors nurture the potential for musical talent and ability.

Developing one's musical talent and abilities is subject to interactionism, that is, social reinforcement between the person and situation (Franzoi, 2009). There is a direct link between one's culture (that is, the person's total life style) and self-motivation. The way in which a person interprets, analyzes, remembers, and uses information is social cognition, which presumably creates a relationship between neural processes of the brain and social processes (termed social neuroscience).

My personal viewpoint, albeit subjective, is that the research supports that everyone has the potential for musical talent, but its development depends on the individual's motivations and commitment, resources and opportunities, and social reinforcement (such as from encouragement from or social modeling after family and friends). Later on, I will discuss this viewpoint extensively.

3

Musical Personality

I have heard numerous people say, "I just don't have the personality to be a musician. You have to be an extravert, plus aren't they all a little crazy?" Comments of this kind and popular stereotypes promulgated by the mass media, although without factual basis, may serve as an unjustified excuse for why a person does not pursue the potential for musicianship.

Contrary to some stereotypes, the idea of an "artist's personality" is not clearly documented by empirical research. As with any other personal choice, such as about how to behave, deciding to engage in music, even if just "singing in the shower," flows from an amalgamation of motives, needs, and personality constructs, as well as sociocultural opportunities that are beyond the prediction or control of the individual (Woody, 1978c, 1999). To say it a bit differently, choosing to have music in your life represents a blend of genetic and biological endowments, along with the social and emotional reinforcement received in life experiences. Throughout this book, I elaborate on this assertion.

Music can fulfill psychological needs. Nietzsche (1974) said: "What is it that my whole body really expects of music? I believe, its own *ease*: as if all animal functions should be quickened by easy, bold, exuberant, self-assured rhythms; as if iron, leaden life should be gilded by good golden and tender harmonies. My melancholy wants to rest in the hiding places and abysses of *perfection*: that is why I need music" (pp. 324–325).

Given the personality composite of biological and social factors, research has not yet answered the question: Why does one person engage in pursuing music and another, perhaps even in the same family (such as a sibling) not do so? Let us consider a few alternative explanations.

Psychoanalytic thought has often addressed creativity, the major component of artistic expression. For example, Storr (1992) summarizes, "As all forms of art depend upon the exercise of phantasy, of the artist's imagination, it is unsurprising that Freud considered that artists are closer to being neurotic than the average person" (p. 91). Freud pointedly links being an artist with a risk for neurosis: "An artist is once more in rudiments an introvert, not far removed from neurosis. He is oppressed by excessively powerful instinctual needs. He desires to win honour, power, wealth, fame and the love of women; but he lacks the means for achieving these satisfactions. Consequently, like any other unsatisfied man, he turns away from reality and transfers all of his interest, and his libido too, to the wishful construction of his life of phantasy, whence the path might lead to neurosis" (Freud, 1963, p. 376).

The foregoing statement seems to intimate that the artist tends toward mental problems, at least in Freud's opinion.

Stated as a question, is being creative linked to psychological difficulties? No, with all due respect to the great Sigmund Freud, there is not adequate empirical research to harbor the idea that creative people are more prone than noncreative people to mental illness (Pavitra, Chandrashekar, & Choudhury, 2007). Moreover, modern thought, even among psychoanalysts, basically repudiates archaic psychoanalytic ideas about creativity and recognizes, on the contrary, the importance of socially reinforced preferences (Gedo, 1989).

Do the youths who engage in music, such as playing or singing in a school ensemble, have different personality characteristics than those who are not in an ensemble? Alter (1989) believes that research supports that, "musicians are different from their peers and that they are autonomous, introverted, highly motivated, and flexible" (p. 185). Yes, there are research studies to support Alter's conclusions, but there are individual differences and idiosyncratic exceptions. Notice how each of the factors cited by Alter has potential relevance to a person's psychological characteristics, including his or her self-concept.

Engaging in music performance means allowing others to observe your characteristics, specifically the music-related behavior but other qualities as well (see the later section on the Naked Musician). Musical composition, arrangement, and performance of any kind require a high degree of personal transparency. If the person has low self-esteem or self-confidence, it is obvious that there might be a reluctance to expose one's self-concept, which could then serve as a deterrent to engaging in any sort of musical experience. Even holing up in the confines of one's practice area, with no intention whatsoever of performing in front of anyone else, requires that the person confront his or her own performance, and if there are self doubts, insecurity, etc., the privacy of practice would not be exempt from critical self-scrutiny.

The Need to be Creative

Connected to the Freudian postulate about a mastery instinct, which has a genetic or constitutional origin, I believe that everyone has some degree of need for and will benefit from expressing creativity. Mastery also connects to the person's ability to control negative emotions and stressful experiences, which promotes health (Surtees, Wainwright, Luben, Wareham, Bingham, & Kraw, 2010). I tend to think of the mastery instinct as a psychological need for originality, that is, to be different from others (as would provide reinforcing distinction for one's unique self-concept) (Woody, 1980, 1984).

Although the biological framework posited by Freud may be questioned, being motivated to fulfill a need for achievement is definite

(McClelland, Atkinson, Clark, & Lowell, 1953). Human nature is such that there is a need to overcome obstacles and master challenges. People vary in the level of their achievement need.

Achievement goal theory holds that the motivation can be task-oriented (mastering a challenge) or ego-oriented (gaining self-esteem from performing well when compared to others) (VandenBos, 2007). Mastery learning is used to gain knowledge and skills: "the acquisition of material beyond basic recognition, recall, and understanding to a point of thorough cognitive integration at a conceptual level" (p. 557).

The research seems to support that there can be great nourishment for the self-concept from mastery learning. From subjective analysis, I have found that recognizing self-accomplishments motivate most people to continue their efforts to be musicians, and the recognition of mastery leads to motivation for follow-up learning (Woody, 2009b). In practical terms, there is great personal reward from mastering a challenge, such as being able to sing or play an instrument.

When compared to people who do not enter into studying music formally, music students seem significantly greater in creativity (Alter, 1989). However, this higher level of creativity could have resulted, to some extent, from what has already been learned, and should not be thought of as a genetic gift.

As I have said earlier, my view is that musical interest and talent are subject to development processes. From childhood musical experiences that move from sheer enjoyment and intuitive expression, there can be a transition to an adolescent devotion to the analytical and formal aspects of music (Bamberger, 1982; Gardner, 1983).

Family Influences

Research makes it clear that an enriched sociocultural background can facilitate an interest in music. Specifically, if the family system and other life experiences (for example, a school music program) promote an interest in music, it is obvious that participants would gain reinforcement to engage in musicianship at some level (Lehmann, Sloboda, & Woody, 2007).

There are two familial thrusts. First, a child's strong instinct-based conviction that parents are ideal people means that a child whose parents engage in music, whether listening or performing, will accept and adopt the parental values about music. Second, there will be social reinforcement from parents who have the resources and motivation to further their child's musicianship. Both of these issues will be discussed in detail later on.

The director of a metropolitan orchestral program for youth reported that, as they drove, she and her young son were listening to a recording of the "New World Symphony," by composer Antonin Leopold Dvořák [1841–1904]. Arriving at their destination, she was about to turn off the motor when her son said, "Mom, can't we wait until this movement is over." Family values can sensitize kids to all music genres.

After the Great Depression, my family was part of the Southern exodus to the northern factories. They brought their limited education, lack of resources, and rural Southern culture with them.

In my childhood family system, neither of my parents and none of my relatives performed music. My father knew three chords on the guitar and could, more or less, play "Red River Valley," "Polly Wolly Doodle," and "She'll Be Comin' Around the Mountain." However, both of my parents enjoyed music on the radio and had a variety of recordings of classical, popular, and country tunes. However, I heard more country and folk music than anything else. [One of my prized childhood memories is spending hours sitting on my father's lap listening to the National Barn Dance and Grand Ole Opry on the Silvertone radio.] Moreover, my mother, who was highly concerned about social standing, thought that music was useful for gaining status. When I was five, my mother paid a quarter for a beat up banjo ukulele, which I would pretend to play now and then.

When I was about seven, a traveling salesman peddling the Oahu Hawaiian Guitar Method came to the door and sold my parents a cheap guitar. He came back a few times to get me started on the Hawaiian guitar. To the pleasure of my family and myself, I did well. I could play recognizable versions of "Redwing," "Nearer My God to Thee," "Bell-bottom Trousers," and a few others tunes.

By the fourth grade, I was consciously aware that I was not a strong student academically (mediocre at best) and thought that the other kids were better than I in almost everything (that is, when it came to peer relations, my self-esteem was not high). The teacher pressed me into playing the Hawaiian guitar at a school assembly. On the same program was the darling of the school, a pretty "older" girl (she was in the fifth grade), who played the "Old Lamplighter" on her accordion. With this experience, I realized that music could offer social acceptance. After all, the old adage says, "You are known by the company you keep," and I was keeping company, so to speak, with one of the most popular girls.

Soon thereafter, the same teacher had me be "conductor" when the class sang for another school assembly. It was not until I was in college that I learned that a basic music education technique is to assign the role of "conductor" to a child who does not sing well. However, being naive, my identity with music gained social reinforcement.

My family and I accepted that my playing a musical instrument could be beneficial. Since the traveling Hawaiian guitar teacher had moved on, I was enrolled in violin lessons and continued sawing away, without much talent, until the end of the eighth grade.

My violin teacher was assistant concert mistress of the Kalamazoo Symphony Orchestra, her husband was a cellist therein as well, and her daughter played the violin. My lessons were in her living room. The sounds of her husband and daughter playing in other rooms, the music piled here and there around the room, and the songs played by the students before my lesson and in recitals attested that my teacher certainly preferred classical music.

Here is the message. My violin teacher realized that, since I was not gifted musically, I needed to be better motivated. Because she knew my family was from the rural South and that I heard country music at home, she made adaptations in the teaching materials. Although I learned formal techniques and played some classical music, she introduced me to fiddle and popular tunes. She also steered me into any youth ensemble that became available.

What the foregoing memory reveals is how life experiences, especially those connected to familial influence, will shape the person's approach to music—regardless of degree of talent. However, as I will talk about later, there are other reinforcement sources that are not within the family per se; peers are a significant influence during adolescence. Indeed, peer reinforcement may be more powerful than parental influence on a person's interests in and ideas about music (Harris, 1998). Also, there is a role for self-determination, based on unpredictable events. I will elaborate on all of these options in later chapters.

4
Musical Sound

Returning to theory about why a person engages in music, there is extensive research establishing that music can arouse the human organism. Neurological arousal impacts on emotions, cognitions, and behavior. Almost like a drug, people whose personality craves stimulation of some kind become rather addicted to experiencing arousal. Depending on the person's neurological system and, later on, his or her social values, music is a potent stimulant for arousal. When among musicians, it is not uncommon to hear a confession, "I'm addicted to music."

Rather than think of this as a negative, satisfying arousal can lead the person into mental and/or physical activity. Alter (1989) explains that the high energy required for musical performance provides intrinsic rewards because: "They may need to release the energy which can become pent up from the fine-tuned control and also, like dance and drama students, they are committed to expending a great deal of energy while engaging in and mastering their musical production" (p. 193).

For example, although there are differences among people and conditions, listening to music (for example, rock versus classical music) may impact study habits and learning (LaVoie & Collins, 1975). With university students (not music majors necessarily), Crawford and Strapp (1994) found that students relying on music during study were more extraverted and reported greater skills in focusing attention and less sensitivity to noise. It appeared that "individuals who choose to study with music may be under-aroused and seek arousal from music in order to be at an optimal performance level" (p. 238).

Music can potentially both enhance and lessen learning. Whether music during a learning effort helps or hinders the acquisition of information seems to be more a matter of the individual's characteristics than a product of volume or type of music. That said, when music was playing, introverts seemed to be most vulnerable to disruption of learning and retention (Daoussis & McKelvie, 1986).

Rather than overgeneralizing, suffice it to say that, as a child develops, being involved with music seems to have a positive influence on academic learning (Gedo, 1989). In turn, the successes or failures experienced by a child in academic learning impact on his or her personality development. Consequently, there is interplay between a student's interest in and exposure to music, effectiveness of learning and academic achievement, and personality characteristics (such as one's self-concept). As I will talk about later on, the foregoing is certainly descriptive of how music changed my approach to academic learning, skill acquisition, personality characteristics, and social relationships.

Generalized Musicianship

As I said at the outset, this book aims to offer information that will allow improvements for beginning and advanced musicians. However, I also noted the goal to help everyday people gain benefits from increasing their musicianship, which I refer to as "generalized musicianship." When considering folks other than musicians per se, the potential for musicianship may, of course, be short of prodigy or artistic level, but it can still promote psychological growth, social relations, and health (Campbell & Doman, 2011; Mannes, 2011).

Aspirations for musicianship must be compatible with one's talents and resources, as well as psychological and physical attributes. Realistic limitations must be identified, acknowledged, and accepted. If the ideal is an impossible dream, the plan to gain musicianship should be tailored to what is possible.

For example, after one semester of graduate school, a performance music major got the message from his primary professor: "You are very good, but you are never going to be a world class performer." Because of an acknowledged need for career security, the student shifted to another (non-performance) music program, earned a doctorate and moved into a successful career.

As another example, although committed primarily to his engineering career, a fine singer applied his analytic mind to his singing and studied how to improve his vocalizing. No, he did not take voice lessons, but being highly intelligent, he read books and articles about singing and listened carefully to recordings. He developed his musicianship to a quality that, had he given up engineering, might have led to professional performances.

An elderly fellow, who started piano lessons after his retirement, told me that focusing on playing the piano was very much the same as how he focused on his golf game. He thought the intensity of the focus was helping him mentally as he advanced in age. That is, his efforts to develop musicianship cultivated his ability to pay attention to details, and he reaped great personal satisfaction from playing the piano daily.

Real-World Conditions

Whatever the mental or physical undertaking, be it music, sports, or work, it is wise to make a conscious commitment to the performance and to seek motivation to improve the quality. The basic psychological principle is that a person has many talents, but each person has limits because of certain real-world conditions.

To reach for one's full potential or to achieve excellence in any talent, more is required. Specific to music, if a person wishes to become exceptionally skilled at music, it is necessary to engage in prolonged study and have ability and temperament to pursue musical expertise (Kemp, 1991). In other words, the old adage "many are called, but few are chosen" comes to mind. A lot of people would like to be excellent musicians. They may even have the potential talent to become outstanding. When they fail to do so, it may not be because of a lack of talent, it may be due to not having the personality characteristics, resources, or opportunity (including being restricted or constricted by other responsibilities, such as earning an income) that would be necessary to develop and maximize their talent.

Musician's Temperament

There have been numerous studies of personality factors that might distinguish musicians from those who choose, consciously or unconsciously, to abstain from music. In a nutshell, there does not seem to be a "musician's personality" per se, but it appears there is a "musician's temperament" (Kemp, 1991; Woody, 1999b).

The results of personality testing may suggest minor or ambiguous differences between musicians and nonmusicians. For example, some studies have found that musicians may tend toward elevated anxiety, perhaps due to insecurity and emotional instability, sensitivity (tendermindedness), and introversion. When trying to point to significant differences, the research does not adequately recognize that there may be variations in temperaments according to the music genre and modality (vocal versus instrumental, and even between different types of instruments); there are research data to support that these ideas are worthy of consideration (Kaufmann &

Rawlings, 2004). Of relevance to my emphasis on the importance of social reinforcements, Kaufman and Rawlings note that learning in a group setting (which offers social reinforcements) may contribute the most to acquiring musical expertise—as opposed to relying on independent practice (which requires sustained self-reliance, tenacity, and precise attitudes about work).

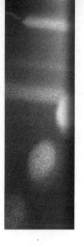

5

Musical Self-Concept

As a threshold for the musical self-concept, it should be recognized that there has been considerable relevant behavioral science research on the self –concept, with the two primary founders of "self" psychology being William James [1842–1920] and George Herbert Mead [1863–1931].

William James was a U. S. psychologist and philosopher, credited by many as being the "father" of psychology. He focused on how emotional identification shapes one's self-concept. It is obvious that music contributes to emotional identification.

George Herbert Mead, a sociologist, did not emphasize emotions. Rather, Mead focused on how the mind and self were inherent to the social process of communications (referred to as the "symbolic interactionist school of psychology") and believed that the self is a product of social interaction or one's role in relationships with others. Each player in the relationship considers the other's perspective (a social exchange), which helps each person understand the rules of the game. For example, the musical interaction between performer and listener is critical to a concert.

Most people think that they are aware of their personal characteristics, saying something like, "I know myself better than anyone else." Regrettably, what seems to be personal insight is often not accurate or realistic. Other people see a person differently, and when they give feedback, whether blatant or subtle, one would think that it would lead the person to have helpful self-understanding. This outcome, however, is not assured as egotism enters the picture.

Defining the Self

If there is any social psychology term that a person should be able to define readily, it would be "self." Everyone goes through life being aware of his or her self. Franzoi (2009) defines the self-concept as, "The sum total of a person's thoughts and feelings that defines the self as an object," and adds that "the self is a symbol-using social being who can reflect on his or her own behavior" (p. 58).

Without getting off track, the term "symbol-using" is certainly apropos for music, given the propensity for certain values and behaviors, brands and models of instruments, and aspirations associated with being a musician. The term symbol-using refers to the how a person relies on cognitions (thinking); symbolic thinking is "the ability to think in terms of signs, symbols, concepts, and abstract relations, as evidence by language, numeracy, and artistic or ritual expression" (VandenBos, 2007, p. 915). Music is, of course, artistic expression. A related term, symbolic representation, "enables the young child to depict and convey ideas through the use of words, sounds, and play" (p. 915) and is "the process of representing experiences in the mind symbolically, for example, through words and sounds"(p. 914). Here again, the words (lyrics) and sounds in music convey information and emotion.

For the musical self-concept, the combination of nature and nurture, talent, motivation, and achievement lead to, produce, and maintain certain personal characteristics. VandenBos (2007) defines the self-concept as follows: "one's conception and evaluation of oneself, including psychological and physical characteristics, qualities, and skills. Self-concepts contribute to the individual's sense of identity over time. The conscious representation of self-concept is dependent in part on the unconscious schematization of the self. Although self-concepts are usually available to some degree to the consciousness, they may be inhibited from representation yet still influence judgment, mood, and behavioral patterns" (p. 828).

The foregoing definition is relevant to the musical self-concept, which I will rely on in explanations and ideas that will help you identify and evaluate your present psychological and physical characteristics, qualities, and skills, as relevant to musicianship. I will guide you to consider these qualities in relation to your personal identity, and examine whether what you believe about yourself is reasonably accurate, how these relevant musical qualities can be changed to your preferences and benefits, and how they connect to your judgments, mood, and behavioral patterns—all within the scope of singing or playing music.

It bears repeating that social psychology involves, "the scientific study of how people affect and are affected by others" (Baumeister & Bushman, 2011, p. 3). Research reveals that music provides people with a way to regulate affect; in other words, the music can change a person's mood (Rippere, 1977). Much more will be said about moods and emotions later. For now, the important point is that, when a performer produces music that is heard by a listener, there is an emotional link established that allows the sound to impact on both of the parties. Thus, performing and hearing music is well within the scope of social psychology.

Musical Communication

From the perspective of social psychology, music is communication. Presumably the communication is from the performer to a listener. However, the musician, such as when practicing, can be both the performer and listener. Even then, the performer is receiving a musical message to him- or herself, such as the emotion instilled or triggered, an appreciation of the technical execution, or a pleasure response from the melody or harmony.

Most often perhaps, a musician expects the communication to be received by someone else, such as friends, family members, or an audience. When there are at least two persons involved in the communication process, social psychology is providing the framework.

There are, of course, countless activities or conditions that will help a person establish and maintain social relationships. In this book, the focus is on music, and how musicianship contributes to the individual self-concept and, consequently, to social relations—and conversely, how social relations influence musicianship.

As evident in the performer-listener link, there are reciprocal effects and benefits. The performer wants to share his or her talents and skills with another person and is rewarded by gaining positive recognition (such as applause) from a listener. If the listener does not like or appreciate the musical effort, the lack of positive reinforcement or the imposition of negative feedback dampens the performer's rewards and musical motivation may be lessened.

The Musical Self-Concept

A person with a well-defined and positive self-concept, as buttressed by a musical identity, will offer enhancing qualities to relationships. In turn, social reinforcements help the individual advance his or her self-concept; links to social reinforcements will be nurturing the individual's quest for a meaningful life, including through music. Moreover, as compared to the multitude of alternatives for self-concept development and strengthening of social relationships, music achieves a unique integration into the person's emotional needs. Emotion and music are inseparable.

Owning Musical Characteristics

To maximize musicianship, the individual should be aware of what music requires of the person (such as the many things discussed earlier), with specific reference to the characteristics that are recognized and "owned" (accepted). Since musicianship generally receives high social acceptance, some people are prone to covet the end product (musical artistry) without being willing to "pay their dues." In other words, they may delude themselves into thinking that they possess more musicianship than reality supports, often feigning celebrity.

In a music store in which I worked during my college years, a teenager spent considerable money regularly ordering big band arrangements, and often talking about performing in Las Vegas. After he had purchased dozens of arrangements, I chanced to ask him about his need for them, and his answer was, "I've never sung in public, but if I ever get the chance, I want to be ready."

It turned out that the young man was somewhat of a social isolate, had no musical background, and harbored a delusion of grandeur about being a celebrity singer with a big band. A sad concomitant was that his parents, who had limited finances, provided him with the money, thinking that buying musical arrangements and pursuing his fantasy would help counter his social isolation and feelings of inadequacy—they were, of course, enabling the delusional disorder.

To develop the musical self-concept, it is essential that the person be realistic about music-related characteristics. It is fine, in fact it is desirable, to have unfulfilled musical aspirations, but to establish a useful plan that will provide dividends for musicianship, one's current state of affairs must be realistic. Much of what is presented in this book is intended to promote accurate and adequate self-awareness.

Social Networks

My analysis of home pages in a major social network reveals a goodly number of claims of music performance that would lead a viewer to believe that the person is an active and celebrated musician. After a web social connection has been established, it becomes evident that the person may have minimal musical accomplishments and has seldom (if ever) performed (for example, a post may say, "playing Bluegrass tonight," and when I back-channel a message about the location of the performance, the person will tell me "on my porch").

Also on social networks, it is not uncommon for a person to adopt the accoutrement (attire, types of instrument, etc.) or talk about contacts with particular celebrities to create a false impression of musical worth. The deluder is, of course, feeding his or her self-concept, even though the nourishment is unhealthy.

There is also reason to believe that a goodly number of folks who engage in social networking indicate that they live in a musical mecca (Nashville, New York, Los Angeles), when they live, in fact, in some other place. And then there is the practice of posting photos from decades before, in an effort to create a youth-based attraction for a fictitious musical self-concept.

Self-Awareness

Human behavior is such that every person potentially has a unique degree of self-awareness—people vary, and musicians are no exception. Neurologically, the frontal lobe of the cerebral cortex (i.e., the anterior cingulate cortex) is activated in high levels of self-awareness (Franzoi, 2009). In addition to human beings, apparently only the brains of great apes and some whales and dolphins suggest that they may possess self-awareness. Whether other species have self-awareness remains for conjecture.

Self-consciousness involves a person engaging in self-awareness on a habitual basis, which is accompanied by heightened concern about the qualities of the self. The concern comes from a discrepancy between private self-consciousness (awareness of the private aspects of the self) and public self-consciousness (what is displayed or made evident to others).

With musicians, it is possible that the end product of performing for others would likely lead to heightened concern about the musical self-concept. This could potentially be a blessing or a curse. Being concerned about one's self-related qualities can strengthen motivation to achieve; however, to make negative self-attributions, which may or may not be realistic, can lead to adverse emotions (such as self-doubt, anxiety, depression, etc.).

The self-concept provides information that allows the person to determine how to behave. Self-regulation is used to control and direct one's actions. Granted, some actions occur automatically; that is, the behaviors are habitual.

Practicing a particular musical exercise or etude over and over and over leads to habituated behavior. Although this can potentially enhance performance quality, there is also the downside that automatic responses may lessen or kill the spark of originality that is of critical importance to artistry.

Just think how difficult it must be for a celebrity to retain his or her musical interest in performing a "hit" or "signature" song throughout his or her career. No doubt "acting" becomes part of the performance. Being on "automatic pilot" likely reduces creativity and motivation for excellence. For musicianship, artistry is generally enhanced when the performer consciously assesses alternatives, such as in improvisation.

Self-Regulation

Studying music with a teacher contributes to development and regulation of the musical self-concept. That is, the teacher helps the student understand what ideas or techniques (such as alternate fingerings, different phrasing, etc.) will elicit from a listener.

When considering self-regulation, psychologists apply "control theory," which contends that "through self-awareness, people compare their behavior to a standard, and if there is a discrepancy, they work to reduce it" (Franzoi, 2009, p. 64). In other words, a person gives consideration to how certain conduct will be viewed or evaluated by others. Also self-awareness allows a person to assess how well personal aspirations or goals are being met.

In developing musicianship, self-regulation processes can reveal a discrepancy between what the person thinks about him- or herself and what he or she would prefer for others to think. Because of the power of social influence, the self-regulation process can contribute positively or negatively to musical aspirations (i.e., defining the ideal self-concept). The self-evaluation can trigger strong emotions, which can also be positive or negative. For example, the musician could experience a sense of dejection, agitation, self-doubt, depression, elation, relaxation, or confidence.

As might be guessed, the process of self-regulation makes demands on the musician's personal resources (Baumeister, Heatherton, & Tice, 1994). Everyone has a quantum of energy that can be devoted to self-regulation, and the musician must guard against depleting his or her reservoir of energy to the point that too little is left for performance excellence.

Thankfully, the personal resources that have been expended will recover over time. In addition to physical factors, the time required for recouping or recovery depends on the particular person's social support system. For example, if a performance on a given night was not particularly successful and the musician anguishes over the outcome, friends and family can bolster the musician for an improved performance the next time. However, if the musician lacks family and friends, the negativity may last for a considerably longer length of time.

Incidentally, the notion that a musician has only a certain amount of energy is strikingly similar to what psychoanalytically oriented psychologists, including Sigmund Freud, have long believed. That is, a person has only so much psychological strength, and when engaging in some sort of psychological effort, such as an exhausting quest for musical excellence or using a defense mechanism to protect one's self or ego (for example, rationalization, denial, etc.), the strength is depleted. To restore or replenish energy, the person must rest or receive rewards (e.g., do an enjoyable activity). Psychological equilibrium must be restored. For example, if a concert is less than satisfying, the musician can "wood shed" (spend more time practicing) and gain ego-related gratification for sensing improved musicianship.

Knowledge Structure for Musicianship

By now in this discussion, it is apparent that the musical self-concept depends on analysis of thoughts and feelings and the assessment of how others respond in interpersonal relationships (for example, how an audience will respond to a performance of a particular composition). Through lessons, practicing, and performances, the musician collects self-information to help regulate his or her behavior and adaptation to the musical situation at hand; and the information is retained in memory for future use.

Musical Self-Schema

As useful for a framework for processing self-related information, conceptualizing a mental structure of one's musical qualities is considered to be a self-schema: "A cognitive structure that represents how you think about yourself in a particular domain and how you organize your experiences in that domain" (Franzoi, 2009, p. 68). A domain is a particular type or category of personal characteristics, such as (along with a few examples) gender (male or female), talents (music, dance, painting, creative writing), family identity (mother, son, cousin), religious preference (Catholic, Protestant, Muslim), and this list goes on and on.

Musical Open-Mindedness

To develop the musical self-concept, whether a beginning student or a professional artist, there must be commitment to changing or improving certain aspects or elements of a self-schema relevant to musicianship. For example, the person might conclude that learning to play a musical instrument would increase his or her feelings of self-worth or impress other people, and so decides to buy an instrument and start taking lessons.

From reviewing social psychology research, I believe that an essential factor, which seems to be often neglected, is that the musician must be open-minded to new information, changing of viewpoints, and acquisition of modified or new values and attitudes (Brown, 2006; Rokeach, 1960, 1973). Having been in music for decades, I am struck by how many vocalists and instrumentalists have done nothing to improve. For example, a vocalist may fail to learn songs in other languages or expand his or her repertoire, or an instrumentalist may have a tone that has not changed for fifty years, plays almost exactly the same "improvised" solos, and sticks to the same list of tunes.

In the realm of closed-mindedness, it is certainly self-defeating to continually sing or play the same songs to an audience that has no culturally developed appreciation for the type of music. A listener or audience will have positive feelings from recognizing and identifying with the musical selection.

It is, of course, one thing to present a composition that reflects a particular era in the genre, but to be unable to shift into other eras is a negative. Similarly, it is one thing to practice and perform exclusively a particular genre or set of compositions, but such limitations may be counterproductive to musicianship.

For example, one classical pianist prides him- or herself on performing the music of the Hungarian composer, Béla Bartók [1881–1945]. Every one of his or her piano students must play Bartók (and little else) and every concert given by the pianist is totally Bartók, rotating through the same compositions year after year after year.

Refinement and quest for excellence of one's chosen repertoire can be honorable, but there can come a point when self-imposed restrictiveness becomes stultifying and reflects close-mindedness. Musicianship is then lessened.

Musical Stereotyping

Music is vulnerable to stereotyping. In other words, people harbor beliefs about personal attributes of a group of people (musicians), which are often overgeneralized, inaccurate, and closed to new information (Myers, 2008). This could lead to thinking, for example, that all or most musicians have certain characteristics or audience members possess particular preferences. Incidentally, since music is emotional (as will be discussed later), this may increase the likelihood of stereotyping.

Returning to the issue of the knowledge structure relevant to musicianship, it is a social psychology principle that a person will be more aware of one's own stereotype-consistent qualities than other people. For example, the musician may painfully remember a bad performance and believe that all future audiences remember the less than sterling past performance. Or the musician may self-identify with a stereotype that "classical musicians are snooty," "jazz musicians are weird," or "country musicians are not good musicians."

Human behavior is such that others tend to retain less memory of a person's past behavior than the person (performer) retains. Others will more readily notice the person's unique qualities at the moment.

Thus, knowledge of a bad past musical performance does not necessarily preordain an audience reaction in the future. In general, listeners are less apt to develop stereotypes about a performance than the musicians themselves. Whether listener or performer, conscious awareness of the possibility of stereotyping can help responsiveness to the actual music-related qualities.

Changes in the Musical Self-Concept

At all stages of life, the musical self-concept fluctuates. From a developmental point of view, a person will value certain things more at one time, say during adolescence, than at another stage of life, say as a senior citizen. Changes in values lead the person to behave differently, which will, in turn, lead to responses from others that are different from what occurred at other stages. For the musician, it is necessary to continue to develop musicianship and avoid the idea that what was desirable at one point in life will always be the preferred.

For example, in popular music, it is well established that, throughout life, most folks tend to retain preference for what was popular during their teenage and early adult years. For the musician, clinging to these "Golden Oldies," that is, popular songs of the past, could be problematic. Think about how the "reunion" shows by once-popular performers often move from a fond memory or nostalgia into realizing how antiquated (dare I say "old"?) the songs or the performers have become (of course, memories and awareness of age can co-exist). Knowledge of or personal preference for music acquired in the (distant) past, should not foreclose seeking new musical knowledge.

The Musical Context

The context in which learning about music occurs will shape qualities that are consistent with the musical self-concept. In varied contexts, the musician will recognize different self-related information, and will potentially receive different feedback depending on the context.

What is "context?" It is "generally, the conditions or circumstances in which a particular phenomenon occurs"; and "in studies of cognition, the environment in which a stimulus event occurs, especially as this influences memory, learning, judgment, or other cognitive processes" (VandenBos, 2007, p. 224). If the musician is limited to a context of formal learning in a school of music, there will be different contextual determinants than if the musician gains knowledge of music from performing in a commercial context, such as in a restaurant or bar.

In retrospect, I realize that I learned a lot because of my having performed music in recital and concert halls, eateries and honky-tonks, hotel ballrooms, radio and television studios, parks and amphitheaters, and on and on. [My favorites "unique" performances were in the "in-field" for a stock car race (when it was so cold there was literally frost on the instruments), and for a bunch of "dignitaries" in a blizzard at the opening of an Interstate exchange (again, it was so cold that valves and keys froze shut).] Each context afforded me with new information relevant to musicianship. Contextual diversity can further musicianship.

The listener's reaction and feedback will also be influenced by the context. For example, how a listener behaves in a sedate concert hall is far different from how the same person will behave—and react to the music—at a rock concert. The contexts are disparate.

The Musical Culture

Earlier, I described how a person's family preferences influence musical interests. Just as context wields a strong influence on the self-concept, so does culture: "the distinctive customs, values, beliefs, knowledge, art, and language of a society or a community" and "the characteristic attitudes and behaviors of a particular group within society, such as a profession, social class or age group" (VandenBos, 2007, p. 250). Cultural heritage has a strong impact on self-concept and will be reflected in opinions, beliefs, and expectations about a variety of things, including music.

If one set of parents enjoys classical music and another set of parents prefers country music, it may seem easy to predict what the preferences of the offspring in the respective households will be. However, a youth can "break" from the family culture. For example, I know that, notwithstanding my parents' predilection for popular and country music, my formal study of music and success as a performer of other types of music led me to put classical and jazz music ahead of other genres. I tell people, "If I am ever marooned on a desert island, I would want either a string quartet or Louis Armstrong playing."

What my varied musical preferences reflect is that everyone has more than one cultural identity, which can lead to cultural frame switching. Since everyone experiences several cultural influences on identity, behavior may switch according to what the context would accept. For example, I demonstrate my cultural heritage differently when I am performing music in a concert for students at a Northern university, as opposed to when I play for my Southern rural kinfolk in their living room. In music, my mindset (what I am cognitively processing and experiencing emotionally) shifts according to the cultural factors relevant to the particular context in which I am performing.

6

Socialized Musical Identity

In the Preface to this book, I mentioned how my personal identity goes beyond the politically correct response of "I'm a father and husband," and does not stop with "I am a professor, psychologist, and attorney." Despite my success and rewards from these other roles, I continue on to say, "I am foremost a musician." That is, my self-concept gives emphasis to my involvement with music.

The self-concept includes various sectors, such as the physical, moral, and social self-concept sectors. In some ways, a sector is like a schema. All sectors are shaped according to social reinforcement, and reflect social identity, which is defined as: "Aspects of a person's self concept based on his or her group memberships" (Franzoi, 2009, p. 75).

Group Memberships

Everyone is a member of several groups. For example, my groups include: my immediate family, the university community, a neighborhood association, professional psychology and law associations, the American Federation of Musicians, and the River City Ragtime Band; and the list contains many other groups.

From the social interactions in each group, I get a certain amount of personal identity and each group imposes a social influence on me. Obviously some groups are more influential than others; and some group influences may impact only one or a few sectors of my total self-concept.

Certainly being a member of a musical ensemble (group) opens the door to considerable social reinforcement. In a community concert band in which I played, it was common to hear the members, most in their middle- or later-years, comment about their fond memories of being in a high school or college ensemble. Musical collegiality, with a shared purpose (e.g., producing a good musical performance), is unsurpassed for potential social reinforcement.

Social Influences and Ethnic Identity

As discussed previously, a person's musical self-concept is subject to social influences. The influences are created by the culture in which the person lives, including ethnic identity. Ethnicity is not simply race, it is: "An individual's sense of personal identification with a particular ethnic group" (Franzoi, 2009, p. 75).

Just so you will know, although ethnicity and race are not one and the same, they are highly similar. VandenBos (2007) tells us that race is: "a socially defined concept sometimes used to designate a portion, or 'subdivision,' of the human population with common physical characteristics, ancestry, or language. The term is also loosely applied to geographic, cultural, religious, or national groups . . . . Moreover, self-reported race frequently varies owing to changing social contexts and an individual's identification with more than one race" (p. 765). Obviously, to believe that race is defined by skin color is an overly simplistic idea.

With the foregoing definitions, it is easy to recognize cultural differences in music. Often the geographical location of the musician is defining, or there could be a framework created by the social values of the area in which the musician lives. It is seldom simply a race-related definition. For example, although certainly influenced by African-American culture, the music of New Orleans is not considered "Black" music—there are numerous other racial groups that have identities within the music from the Big Easy; and the music from that area crosses into a variety of genres, far more than Dixieland jazz.

To develop musical identity, the musician should not ignore his or her ethnicity-related origins, influences, and motivations. Musicianship is enhanced by exploring and seeking increased understanding of the meaning of ethnicity for oneself, and hopefully acquiring a clear and confident ethnic sense—and then internalizing the ethnicity factors into the creation, formulations, and performances relevant to music. Review the various comments that I have made about how I became a musician, and notice how often there were powerful ethnic factors present.

The bottom line is that, in one's search for self-understanding, as would contribute to a well-defined musical self-concept, consideration should be given to one's ethnicity. A sense of ethnicity can contribute positively to healthy self-understanding.

The Naked Musician

No, I do not intend to suggest that you perform without clothing (although certain performers have been known to do it!). However, it is a fact that performing music for other people to witness is very revealing. Given the importance of listeners to the musical self-concept, exposing one's artistry to others requires stripping away any accoutrements of guardedness of self-concept.

Impression Management

Everyone has some degree of concern about how he or she is seen (perceived) by others. Almost constantly and regardless of the context, each of us tries to shape or influence how others see us.

Through clothing, conduct, choice of instruments, musical selections, and on and on, a musician is continually engaged in "impression management" for "strategic self-presentation." These efforts can lead to positive regard from listeners and within the musician, or there can be negative fallout from failure to be effective in impression management.

Failures in impression management bring on unwanted responses from others. In Nashville, it is common to see someone on the street using a western hat, boots, embroidered shirt, and the like to emulate the appearance of a particular celebrity for whom there is idolatry. It is doubtful that others provide a positive response to this type of attempt (it is more likely that a negative attribution occurs).

For another example of faulty impression management, one community choir conductor does a good job with the music itself, but does not communicate well in her relationships with choir members. Consequently, the turnover of members is more than would be best. Moreover, the director tends to interrupt the musical flow at concerts, and launch into a long-winded discourse that emphasizes her own needs and virtues. She believes that her approach fosters a positive impression. Suffice it to say, her impression management is low-grade because of her lack of sensitivity to how others react.

Self-Presentation

It is not easy to manage self-presentation effectively. In fact, the challenge can be stressful, because it requires energy, self-analysis, decision-making, and actions that may or may not be easily accomplished.

The mass media portray certain images about what is good or bad in a male or female at a certain age or stage of life. If the person attempts to live up to the endorsed or portrayed good image, it may require qualities or characteristics that are difficult or impossible to obtain, be it on occasion or consistently. Failure to satisfy the good image can then have a negative (stressful) impact on the person's sense of self-worth. With musicians, there may be a lack of personal self-awareness (as with the aforementioned "Broadway Cowboys/girls" and community choir director) or a constricting personality (such as a lack of open-mindedness to adopting improved musical skills, communication, and conduct).

Being Sensitive to the Listener

Exposing the musical self-concept requires a realistic appraisal of what will be well received and perceived by a listener or an audience (or within one's self). In other words, after considering and defining the judgmental sources (the targeted listeners) relevant to the musician's qualities, the next step is to surmise a set of characteristics expected to be aligned with the listening sources.

For example, whether the audience is "youthful" or "more mature" should shape the musician's decision-making about what to reveal (such as dress, talk, musical selections). I am aware that when the River City Ragtime Band plays on a college campus, the response to a sing-along request will be quite different than if it were made in a senior residential facility—college-age people are not likely to know the lyrics to songs from seventy-five years ago. From elementary school, today's college students might remember "Puff, the Magic Dragon" or "This Land is Your Land," but it is highly doubtful that they, like a more senior audience, would know the lyrics to "I'm Looking Over a Four-Leaf Clover" or "Hello, Dolly."

The foregoing reflects that, once the listeners' expected characteristics have been formulated, there must be an assessment of the risks involved with and the emotions that will be aroused by the performance. For example, if there is reason to believe that a given audience will not favor a certain type of musical performance (that is, the context is not desirable for the type of music that would be performed), it may be best for the musician to say, "thanks, but no thanks" to the opportunity to perform and thereby avoid a clash of musical preferences.

A leader of a touring ensemble makes a point of reading about the history of a community in which a performance is scheduled. In addition to making historical comments during the actual performance (which promotes a positive "shared identity" between the audience and ensemble), the "play list" (i.e., the music selected for the program) is tailored to the community's current demography.

For anyone and especially a musician, knowing from experience what makes for effective self-presentation creates a guide. The full benefits of self-gratification and career success hinge on gaining social acceptance from others (such as listeners).

Ingratiation is one self-presentation strategy, and involves trying to shape others' impression through flattery. Research supports that the recipient of ingratiation is likely to respond positively to flattery. However, caution must be exercised to avoid cynicism, as might come from a performer overdoing the flattery. That is, an audience might think that the positive comments from a musician ("You are one of the finest audiences for whom I have performed . . .") are mere pap, something said to every audience. The comments should not raise a question about the motive.

It is a rare situation that allows a performer, even a comedian, to ridicule an audience and not get a negative reception in return. Negativity or criticism of another person is distasteful and creates defensiveness and rejection.

For a musician, it is much more logical to choose "shared identity" as an impression management tool. For example, one fine musician mentions tactfully that there is a "friendly connection" between herself and those in the audience, such as saying "You are so kind with your smiles and applause, I sure wish you all lived in my neighborhood."

Avoiding Self-Aggrandizement

All too often, it seems that performers harbor the false notion that acceptance will be gained by citing all of their great qualities. To the contrary, modesty is effective in increasing likeability and preserves high levels of perceived competence and honesty.

Self-promotion, such as describing one's artistic credentials in detail or bragging about past performances and praise from critics, can be a double-edged sword. Tactfully presenting musical assets and accomplishments may result in an attribution about likeability, charm, intelligence, or talents, but there is also the risk that the other person(s) will be turned off and believe that the self-promotion reflects insecurity or narcissism.

One jazz guy could not converse with other musicians without bragging about how his musical abilities and views were far superior to anyone else's. He was, of course, indicating implicitly that he was superior to them. Audiences were well aware that he was a braggart, and some listeners sensed that he was disliked by fellow musicians (through grimaces and other nonverbal cues). Of course, a number of musicians declined to perform with him because of his braggadocio. Despite being an excellent musician, with impressive mastery of his instrument, his career did not flourish, which was clearly due to his insensitive self-promotion.

One classical musician talked in a demeaning way to other musicians in a jazz/popular ensemble, suggesting that she was "slumming" by playing in their group. This is maladaptive behavior, which I refer to as "cultural snobbery."

Regrettably, I have seen the self-aggrandizement many times with musicians from all musical genres. More than once, the leader of an ensemble has had musicians quit because of an obnoxious egocentric member. As might be expected, the self-aggrandizing musician evokes negative reactions from colleagues and audiences alike. Suffice it to say, the musician who acts in the foregoing manner is revealing his or her character deficits and lack of social skills and sensitivity.

Ironically, instead of one-upsmanship, research supports that a better strategy for winning favor with listeners (and fellow musicians) is one-downsmanship. The idea is that the musician with a well-defined and healthy self-concept can communicate modesty and recognition of others' positive qualities. For example, simply starting a sentence with "As you probably know already," creates equality between the personal musician-listener, avoids self-defensiveness within the listener, and leads to a positive set for receiving the information (such as liking the comments or music).

Positive Exemplification

For revealing the musical self-concept, it should be remembered that "the proof is in the pudding." Exemplification involves trying to prove one's qualities by actual performance. This strategy lets the other person(s) make a judgment. Psychologically, a person likes to believe that he or she is self-determining, which leads to a tendency to weight the determination positively. For example, the listener is apt to be more positive by self-determining a judgment of the musical effort than trying to be convinced by bragging from a performer.

Even in the framework of exemplification, sensitivity is necessary. A fine musician might well be able to perform in a fashion superior to others, but by not "fitting in" would receive negativity. As any erstwhile musician knows, the hallmark of musicianship is being about to perform in a manner that will improve the overall ensemble sound and, ideally, bring out the best in fellow musicians.

Self-Handicapping

Self-handicapping is an inept strategy to try to gain sympathy or get the bar lowered for musical performance by admitting one's shortcomings. An admission of personal limitations is one thing, but it can also look like trying to avoid responsibility for the work, effort, standards, or quality expected or reflected because of personal insecurity. When a musician tells an audience about not feeling well, having a faulty instrument, the poor acoustics in the concert hall, the bad sound system, etc., it may be an inept attempt to gain listener support through self-handicapping comments.

Sometimes the musician consciously or unconsciously sets him- or herself up to fail. Thus, the definition for self-handicapping states: "A self-presentation strategy in which a person creates obstacles to his or her own performance either to provide an excuse for failure or to enhance success" (Franzoi, 2009, p. 81).

Failing to practice adequately before a lesson or a performance is also self-handicapping. Another common problem, not unique to musicians per se, is for the person to become intoxicated or abuse some substance to a degree that it decreases musical competency.

Self-Monitoring

In the baring of the musical self-concept, impression management requires constant self-monitoring, which involves noting, assessing, and altering cues from other people's reactions. Since self-promotion strategies are used to hopefully gain positive reactions from others, it is not surprising that the musician needs to take stock of relevant conditions and influences. Research supports that: "High self-monitors are highly attuned to social cues and readily alter their self-presentations to match the current situation. Low self-monitors are relatively inattentive to social cues and their behavior is guided more by their attitudes and beliefs" (Franzoi, 2009, p. 85).

Musicians who are effective at self-promotion are thought to be high in monitoring, whereas those who avoid the process are considered to be low in monitoring and prone to be inept socially. Obviously the musician wishing to promote success should strive to be a high self-monitor. This quality is an important asset for the musical self-concept.

Evaluating the Musical Self-Concept

Monitoring extends to awareness and assessment of social conditions and influences. To maximize benefits in social contexts, the musical self-concept should maintain efforts for realistic self-appreciation.

The term self-esteem refers to personal evaluations. If the musician has a low opinion of him- or herself, success is unlikely. On the contrary, cultivating a positive—but realistic—degree of self-esteem is invaluable for gaining positive outcomes.

Throughout the course of a day, every person makes many self-evaluations. Information for consideration comes from a wide variety of sources, some real, some imaginary. The person who is realistic and secure is the most likely to have evaluations that are reliable and valid. Not surprisingly, people who have low self-esteem are commonly more unhappy, pessimistic, and achieve less in life than those folks who have reality-based high self-esteem.

Self-esteem may also connect to the person's commitment to healthy behaviors and longevity. Put into a musical framework, a musician who creates realistic and healthy self-esteem will be the most apt to have musical longevity.

Self-esteem is vulnerable to the old saw "too much of a good thing." The musician may experience a negative effect from unrealistic and unhealthy high self-esteem, especially if it is infiltrated by flights into fantasy (i.e., notions of false competency).

If the person's self-esteem lacks stability, it is probable that anger and hostility will erupt when his or her self-worth is challenged. In turn, it may be difficult or impossible for the person to control these negative reactions—which could lead to adverse results, such as being rejected by others and suffering destruction of musicianship.

For example, one leader of a touring ensemble was quite insecure psychologically, yet tried to convey that he was at an ultra-level of artistry. Whenever a member of the ensemble would perform in a way that was obviously superior to the leader's ability, the leader would not, either on or off stage, offer commendations. Instead, there would be an angry tirade by the leader (off stage), denouncing the noteworthy ensemble member. Needless to say, there was an immediate parting of the ways between the two of them.

With that ensemble, there was a long list of musicians who had exited because of the leader's propensity for insecurity and anger. Other musicians in the community viewed the leader as a volatile personality and one who was not a desirable source for affiliation.

If the person's explicit self-esteem (what is conscious and deliberate in the self-evaluation) is discrepant (not in syncrony) with his or her implicit self-esteem (what is unintentional and perhaps unconscious in the self-evaluation), it may be an indicator of a character disorder, such as a person with an unrealistic high self-evaluation (i.e., narcissism). In other words, the aforementioned leader's implicit self-evaluation was quite low, albeit denied (unconscious?), and the highly explicit self-esteem was but a façade (he exaggerated and falsified his accomplishments, such as where he had obtained musical training and the musical accolades that he had received). More will be said about character disorders in a later chapter.

In social psychology, the self-evaluation maintenance model holds that self-esteem is potentially enhanced by social relationships and social comparisons (matching, complementing, or surpassing performances by others). Self-awareness, self-monitoring, the self-schemas (the hypotheses or notions one has about personal qualities), self-regulation, and self-esteem are the dimensions for the musical self-concept and are linked to socialized identity.

7

Music Performance and Interpersonal Interactions

The foregoing discussion considered establishing a positive reception from listeners (e.g., an audience) and other musicians. Now comes a topic for which everyone—at all ages—commonly has a strong interest, namely interpersonal interactions.

Relationships are influenced by social attraction, which refers to experiencing a desire to come in contact or communicate with other people. In other words, being attracted to someone leads to a wish and openness to engaging in social relations.

As I have mentioned, some musicians are reluctant or resistant to exposing their musical nakedness to others, and are content and prefer to stay isolated in the practice room savoring the music alone. There is, of course, nothing "wrong" with doing music for oneself, but becoming socially isolated can be detrimental to mental health, and since social relations can offer positive reinforcement, isolation can stifle creativity and thwart musicianship.

Social Anxiety in Musicianship

Some musicians who prefer psychologically to stay in their private world (social introversion) may experience varying degrees of tension and anxiety when conditions require them to be exposed—as occurs with stage fright (performance anxiety), which may erupt from unconscious or unacknowledged self-doubts. Sometimes the performance anxiety comes if the musician has unrealistically highly expectations that are impossible to achieve. Of course in artistry, it can also be said that, when one becomes satisfied with the level performance that is obtained, the person's musical quest has been diminished.

I have encountered numerous musicians with strong devotion to their musicianship, but because of their faulty self-concept and inability to be comfortable in social relations, they become isolated socially. Several come to mind who could be reasonably comfortable and able when playing in an orchestra, in which they are assigned to a particular seat and instrumental part, and the expectancies for attire and conduct are clear—but they could not converse or interact outside of the well delineated space, role, and functions that exist in a rehearsal or performance of an orchestra. This set of circumstances is not genre-specific. Of course some of the other musicians tended to think of these introverted musicians as "just plain weird." Since this kind of response is likely communicated in one way or another, enriching social relationships and the interactions therein will probably not happen.

People Who Need People

Regardless of culture, people have a primary (deep-seated) psychological need to be involved and interact with other people in a positive manner. There are many reasons; in a positive relationship, there are allies who will help with survival, share resources, and offer emotional support.

Famed psychologist, Harry Frederick Harlow [1905–1981], who did comparative research (comparisons of humans with certain animal species), found that there is an inherent need for contact comfort, that is, reassurance from a gentle touch (Blum, 2002). In the musical experience, the "gentle touch" may be fulfilled vicariously—the audience being nurtured (touched) by the performance, and the musician being reinforced (touched) by the smiles and applause from the listeners.

When the statement, action, conduct, or performance is for either or both emotional (applause) and/or material/instrumental (financial income from bookings to perform) rewards, it is referred to as fulfilling a psychological need for affiliation. The affiliative motivation or drive plays out in efforts to form friendships, attachments, and interactions. The latter would include being accepted into a musical ensemble or simply being identified with other musicians. Recalling the comments about the misleading information posted on social networks, this may have an underlying affiliative or affiliation motivation to be seen as a member of the world of music (group).

To a large extent, social affiliation offers emotional security (that is, to avoid feeling anxious or frustrated): "Although individuals differ in the strength of their desire to be with others, stressful situations typically intensify the need for affiliation; this is especially so when these others are undergoing the same stress, perhaps because being part of a group helps to reduce the unpleasantness of the situations" (VandenBos, 2007, p. 27). As mentioned earlier in the book, there is reason to believe that, notwithstanding the need for affiliation, musicians may be prone to be more introverted than commonly expected (Woody, 1999b).

Social Comparisons Among Musicians

When people meet or come together, there is a social comparison. For example, if a musician joins a musical ensemble, his or her thoughts and actions are compared to what are presumably possessed by others in the group. Of course, the presumptions may not be accurate in either self-assessment or about what another person seems to possess.

Social Exchanges Among Musicians

Interpersonal reinforcement is relevant to the social exchange. As with all sorts of human behavior, the person is prone to seek and maintain relationships that provide rewards that are greater than the expenditure of effort or other resources.

In addition to an activity (practicing or performing) or interpersonal interactions, and as strange as it may seem, the social relationship can be with or through a musical instrument; that is, the instrument itself becomes part of vicarious social reinforcement. Think of how some musicians give a personal name to their musical instrument, such as B. B. King's [1925-   ] famous guitar "Lucille." Victor Wooten (2006) mentions talking to one's instrument. Although seemingly a reflection of anthropomorphism (Horowitz & Bekoff, 2007), the personalization of the musical instrument, consciously or unconsciously, feeds into the wish for social interactions. For example, musicians often practice in front of a mirror. There is potential social reinforcement from engaging in any of the aspects of musicianship.

When it comes to deciding to pursue music, the idea of reinforcement from and valuing the reactions of others is nothing new. More than a century ago, a primogenitor of behavioral psychology, Edward L. Thorndike [1874–1949] said: "Any act which in a given situation produces satisfaction becomes associated with that situation, so that when the situation recurs the act is more likely than before to recur also" (Thorndike, 1905, p. 203).

Any opportunity that evoked a positive response to a musical performance, such as for listeners, will have appeal. One couple told me how their social organization had a waiting list of musical groups who would play for little or nothing, just for the opportunity of performing. A musician told me, "I an ecstatic when I get a chance to have someone else appreciate my music."

In a sense, the foregoing reinforcement principle is the basis for social exchange theory, but with some differences. Thibaut and Kelley (1959) do not believe that having rewards that exceed the costs is the primary motive for staying in a relationship. Instead, they believe that the person will evaluate the current relationship for rewards and costs, but will rely on whether there are other options for a relationship that may be better. If there is no better alternative, the person will stay in the current relationship, even if it has an unattractive rewards-costs evaluation.

It must be acknowledged that, in addition to actual social interactions, the musical self-concept receives intrapsychic rewards. For example, the emotional payoff for the musician from just practicing alone is reinforcing. One wife said, "I want my husband to practice each day because it wards off grumpiness." Numerous musicians have admitted, "I don't feel like I am complete unless I am practicing my music." At some level, the musician is, however, using the practicing as a means for conjuring up, again consciously or unconsciously, the possibility of gaining rewards from social interactions in the future.

For a musician, even if performances are not going well, having invested the time and energy (and motivational aspirations) in music and not having any other career options, the lackluster musician may continue on pursuing the impossible dream. However, if he or she becomes trained for a new career, commitment to music may be altered.

I did not forecast great success for myself as a performing musician, but was still rewarded by it. I was blessed with opportunities to develop competency (successively) in education, psychology, health care, and law. Through it all, I retained my passion for music but was obviously getting greater rewards (measured by income and professional recognition) from my other (nonmusical) endeavors. Still, however, I play my instruments daily and perform for others.

Inadequate Affiliations

It is axiomatic that people commonly have a need to "belong," that is, to be affiliated with others. If a person does not adequately satisfy (fulfill) the affiliative or affiliation need through social relations, such as due to being disliked, rejected, or excluded, the person may react in a variety of negative ways, such as experiencing increased stress, anxiety, diminished self-esteem, and self-defeating thinking and behavior.

This sort of negativity can have devastating psychological and physical effects. For example, without positive social relationships, the musician may become weakened emotionally, and develop mental difficulties and psychosomatic (mind-body interaction) conditions.

Also, it is possible that a dearth of fulfillment of the affiliation need will lead the musician toward further maladaptive avoidance responses (becoming reclusive, having less motivation to practice or perform) or maladaptive approach responses (engaging in harmful behaviors, like substance abuse). For musicianship to flourish, nourishing affiliations are required.

Arousal of a person's central nervous system (CNS), the complex connection involving the brain and spinal cord, results in positive and negative emotions being experienced (Campbell & Doman, 2011). The late British psychologist, Hans Jürgen Eysenck [1916–1997] conducted research that suggested that introverts (people who are reclusive) may have inherited a CNS (brain and spinal cord) that requires more arousal than is required by extroverts (people who are outgoing).

People vary in their tolerance for the stimulation that comes from social interaction, which leads to differing emotional responses (Eysenck, 1990). Stated bluntly, this notion supports that biological factors shape our affiliation needs. Also, as said several times, a musician with a propensity for introversion, which seems to be reasonably common among musicians, may well be operating with a genetic endowment.

It is important to realize that life is not totally determined by heredity. Recall the earlier discussion of nature versus nurture. Beyond biology, our cultural and social experiences reinforce affiliation tendencies. Even something as profound as gender will be shaped to some degree by one's roles within social relationships. As a bottom line, efforts for optimum musicianship will be reinforced by positive social relationships.

Situational Conditions and Attraction

Interpersonal attraction depends on a wide variety of factors and conditions. There is no set of prescriptions or proscriptions relevant to attraction. However, there are certain conditions that seem important to musicianship, albeit there could be others included as well.

Closeness

The term "propinquity" refers to: geographic space, close or distant, between two or more people to each other. Research reveals that living close together leads to greater personal acceptance, such as between next-door neighbors compared with someone who lives on the next block.

The study of "proxemics" considers interpersonal special behavior relevant to propinquity. Here are a couple of examples involving proxemics with musicians.

Just by chance, Musician A moved next door to Musician B. They had not known each other before. Among musicians in the community, Musician B had a long-term reputation of being hard to get along with, and some musicians refused to perform with him or her because of abrasiveness. However, for about twenty years living next door to each other, Musician A and B never had a disagreement, including during countless performances that they did together.

As another example, it is not uncommon to find music educators in the same department or members of an ensemble being thrust into close and frequent contact in a given physical context, even though they have significant differences in personal characteristics. The differences would be great enough that, in another context that did not require or enforce close contact, there could even be disliking and oppositional behavior. However, because of their shared objectives, such as maintaining effective music education or creating a fine performance, there is contextual compatibility. For example, a prominent musical director was described as being an extremely volatile, profane, insulting, and angry person in social situations in the home city, but when he was on the road for a celebrity's tour, he was "sweet, easygoing, and a pleasure to have leading our ensemble."

From social psychology research, it can be assumed that people who, perhaps by chance circumstances or mandate (like the two next-door musician-neighbors described earlier), are in close proximity are likely to have positive acceptance of each other. The principle is, of course, simple: being "forced" to be in close proximity leads to a conscious or unconscious awareness of the need to get along with each other; people may tend to downplay differences and see (perhaps even exaggerate) the importance of similarities. When it comes to friends or musical associates with whom they share close physical space or context, propinquity can lead musicians to, quoting an old song, "accentuate the positive and eliminate the negative."

Exceptions to Closeness

Certainly there can be exceptions to the effects of closeness. The proximity or propinquity principle supports that neighbors should get along well with each other. However, when some unfortunate incidents occur that lead to animosity or disliking, the negativity can continue even though the folks are living, say, right next door to each other. When this occurs, there is a good chance, however, that one or more of the people will also have personal characteristics that are causing and maintaining the dissonance or there has been a change in the rewards that kept the relationship going.

Notwithstanding propinquity or a shared enterprise, there can be personal characteristics that negate a positive relationship. Earlier examples were given of personal characteristics that impacted negatively on the musicians in a group.

In a concert band, the low brass section had only one female member. The other members of the section openly derided her musicianship, even suggesting that the conductor eliminate any solo passage that might be in her part; on occasion, such alterations were made to her part without her knowledge. She told me how the other section members had railroaded other players to get them out of the band, and how she sometimes left rehearsals with tears in her eyes.

In this example, it remains for conjecture as to whether the female member had problematic characteristics, either in terms of her personality or musicianship, or whether what occurred was so-called *folie à groupe* (which involves irrational ideas and bigotry) shared by the male members of the section. In any case, the negative interactions did not reflect well on anyone and certainly did not advance musicianship.

Incidentally, it has been found that, when there is a negative reaction between people entering a relationship, those same nay-sayers may later on become the staunchest of supporters, more than seems logical. The reason traces to the notion that each person has judgmental credibility, they are discerning and choosey about with whom they form a relationship. In other words, just because two musicians may not have a positive initial reaction to each other does not mean that there will always be disliking and, in fact, they may become staunch allies.

In one major music mecca, it is a common joke that almost all newly formed groups will break up soon. All too often, musicians who got along well back in the hinterland make the move to the "Magic Town" as a group, but when they fail to find musical stardom, they start fighting among themselves. Inevitably, they dissolve the group, and if they stay in the city, they may bad-mouth each other for years to come.

The two foregoing examples reveal that personal closeness is not always a given or sustainable. With the lack of reward from social affiliation and shared career endeavors, interpersonal negativity erupts.

Magnificent Obsessions

Positive social interactions require that each person be realistic about what the relationship can provide. The investment of the self-concept in the shared enterprise deserves comment.

A rock group practiced diligently and seemingly had a cohesive group. As they improved, it was apparent that each musician started developing a sense that fame was coming soon—it grew to the level of an obsession for everyone in the band.

Collectively the band members reasoned that they were getting so good that, if they had one big concert, it would be a springboard to the national scene. Each band member invested money, time, and ego in equipment, advertisements, facilities, etc. (a focus that created friction on their "day jobs" and with family members).

The night of their initial concert came and the event fell with a thud. Each member blamed the others for the lack of success. Because there was so much egotism invested, each band member experienced a disruption in emotional stability. They started bickering with each other. Within a few days after the long anticipated chance to catapult to fame that was not to be, the band broke up permanently. After just one concert, the band dissolved because of faulty self-concepts and irrational ideas, or so it would seem. Besides leaving the group, the "leader" soon divorced (happenstance?).

Regardless of the musical genre (be it classical, jazz, rock, popular, country, or whatever), the social psychology principle is the same. If an ensemble or group comes to harbor an obsession that lacks grounding in reality, and then does not achieve the psychological and career payoffs that were motivating forces, there will likely be dissonance among the members—there will be rationalizations, blaming, distancing, and breakup.

Interdependence

Another social psychological principle associated with positive interpersonal interactions is that experiencing anxiety or stress increases a person's need for affiliation. This principle is derived, to a large extent, from the research by Leon Festinger [1919–1989], known for his theory of cognitive dissonance, and Stanley Schacter [1922–1997], known for research on social motivation. The two basic notions are: (1) people are motivated to maintain consistency, and inconsistency will lead to attitude or behavioral changes to eliminate the mental dissonance; and (2) the motivating factors within social comparisons (considering the emotional reactions of others) lead to dependence on others.

In a situation that is potentially embarrassing for a person, such as performing music for an audience, there may be a tendency to handle the stress by affiliating with others who do not know about the impending embarrassment. If the situation creates fear, the person may tend to affiliate with others who have gone through the same kind of situation, thereby gaining "cognitive clarity" (obtaining information about the nature and dangerousness of the threat). For example, if Musician A, a pianist, has anxiety about (fear of) being embarrassed by a faulty solo performance, hearing Musician B talk about having decided to be a piano accompanist instead of a soloist, Musician A might be prone to become friends with Musician B.

Reduced to a psychological principle, research supports that stress, whether due to an event (a performance than went awry) or a personal characteristic (low self-esteem), will motivate the person to increase affiliations in order to gain information that might allay the stress. In retrospect, I realize that the camaraderie that commonly existed between students when I was majoring in music, working on a doctorate, or pursing a law degree, was fostered by this psychological principle. Wishing to avoid failure in one's studies is relevant to the old saw, "Us against them" (students versus the faculty), or perhaps there is a touch of "misery loves company."

Physical Attraction

Most everyone knows that physical attractiveness is important for social relationships. There is, however, a misconception that physically attractive individuals, when compared to less attractive people, have greater socially desirable personality traits and happier lives.

Physical attractiveness does seem to bring about rewards, but it is no guarantee of overall success. For example, attractive people often gain preference from others, including in educational experiences (there are attributions of capability) and employment situations (relied upon for hiring, salary, and promotion decisions). To some degree, this principle certainly extends to musical efforts.

For example, among others, consider the number of commercial female instrumentalists who dress in exotic gowns or musical ensembles that (perhaps not admittedly) select physically attractive members. In "show biz," everyone wants to be beautiful. Yes, physical attractiveness is probably an asset, but as said already, it is no guarantee of success for musicianship in general.

In a meta-analysis (lumping a batch of research studies into one analysis), Feingold (1992) found that that beautiful folks do not necessarily have more desirable personality traits, such as intelligence, dominance, self-esteem, and mental health. However, other research suggests that a self-fulfilling prophecy may lead to the attractive person's confirming stereotyped expectations. Franzoi (2009) believes: "The apparent reason physically attractive people tend to be socially poised and confident is that those who interact with them convey the clear impression that they truly are very interesting and sociable individuals" (p. 352).

To be sure, contemporary society places a premium on physical attractiveness. There is no doubt that modern times offer countless indications of great emphasis being placed on attractiveness, perhaps enhanced by fashions and other adornments. In the entertainment industry, physical attractiveness often outweighs talent. Some musical Super Stars (no names mentioned) have only a modicum of musical ability or talent, but because of their attractiveness—along with astute management and promotion—they are heralded as performers. Research suggests the emphasis on attractiveness is applied more to females than for males.

For the musical self-concept, the musician should seek to develop so-called "body esteem," which is relevant to the level of physical and social self-concept that can be attained. There should be no denial of reality. If a musician is frail or obese, it makes no sense to distort or deny the attributes; the rational solution is to seek improved dietary, fitness, and other considerations (perhaps with medical guidance). It is common knowledge these days that physical fitness and health complement musical competency. In fact, numerous professional musicians report efforts to be physically fit are considered to be part of developing musicianship because of increased stamina and energy for performing with gusto.

Balance Theory

By now, it has been said several times that people like consistency, and any time when there is dissonance (such as between beliefs), an attempt is made to resolve the discrepancy. For example, if a musician is told by a teacher that his or her chance of being successful is poor, the musician, if he or she has a significant psychological investment in a music career, will experience dissonance between aspiration and prediction—and will set about to resolve the dissonance. The musician might rationalize that the teacher is naïve and not a true authority or, in the alternative, settle down and practice more to gain reassurance for his or her career plan.

In social psychology, balance theory holds that people wish for or need cognitive consistency in their thoughts, feelings, and social relationships. A balanced relationship means that the people involved with each other value the same thing. In an unbalanced relationship, the people would be dissimilar, such as in their attitudes, values, and beliefs. Yes, "birds of a feather should flock together."

Shared attitudinal characteristics appear to be more important than similar personality characteristics at the attraction (early) stage of forming a relationship. Once involved in a relationship, there is a shift in influences, and there may be greater importance placed on having similar personalities (to avoid the conflicts that could lessen satisfaction within the relationship).

In music projects, the shared attitudes about type of music, lyrical dimensions, repertoire for a particular instrument, etc., can lead musicians to create social relationships with each other. The fact that the musicians are different in other spheres of life (such as religion, politics, race, and so on) is secondary or minimally relevant to the primary shared basis of the social relationship—music.

A good example comes from the early years of jazz. Frequent commentators credit the shared attitudes about jazz as helping musicians of different races come together, and in the long run the racial integration extended to the audiences. The risk of imbalance can be minimized by conscious acceptance that the primary basis of a relationship between musicians has a connection to musicianship.

Social psychology research supports that after awhile the similarity in beliefs and values may be overshadowed by differences in personality characteristics, and if the dissimilarity is too great, their social attachment may deteriorate or be severed. For example, among musicians there may be disputes that, although not connected to music per se, lessen the comfort with and rewards from the music-based connections.

Of course there are always exceptions. For example, if one of the persons in a musical relationship continues to like the other person (such as being enamored by some charismatic quality), the relationship may continue, notwithstanding significant differences in personality characteristics.

In a touring ensemble (described earlier), the leader alienated one member after another, so there was considerable turnover of personnel (which affected the quality of performance). No matter what negatives the cantankerous leader threw at them, two members stayed. In talking with them, it was apparent that they thought the leader was an exceptional instrumentalist and to be affiliated with someone of such outstanding musical ability led them to discount his tirades and condemnations. In turn, the leader's ego was massaged, so to speak, by this unique and continued acceptance by the two musicians.

Problematic Social Interactions

When a musician is concerned about how he or she is being evaluated by another person in a musical relationship, there is the possibility of the unpleasant emotions from social anxiety. Anxiety from an event tends to increase the wish to affiliate with potentially supportive sources.

When the anxiety is due to other people, real or imagined (such as criticism from others in an ensemble), the tendency is to withdraw from most or all interpersonal contact. Stated differently, being socially anxious makes it less likely that the person will initiate or continue contacts or communications with people, conditions, or contexts perceived as triggering the discomfort. Recall the example of the community band section that criticized the only female member's musical ability; it was not long before she dropped out and transferred to a similar ensemble in a nearby community in which the other people provided encouragement, not negative comments.

Avoidance and Withdrawal

To avoid negatives, a person is likely to withdraw from or end interpersonal interactions. This likelihood tends to be greatest when the other person is unknown or distrusted. Said differently, if there is familiarity with a person, even if there are negatives in the interactions, avoidance and withdrawal are relied upon less often. In and of itself, familiarity offers a certain degree of solace, security, and reinforcement in interpersonal interactions.

Among musicians, there may be a tendency to avoid or withdraw from interactions with musicians with whom there is limited familiarity. For example, one fellow acknowledged that "sticking with the same band is not satisfying, but I'm unsure about how other musicians in town would consider my playing."

A social psychology principle relevant to avoidance and withdrawal posits that, within social relationships, there will be less tolerance of negative conditions from a new source, as compared to a source with whom there has been a long-term connection. Recall how, because of propinquity and the passage of years, Musician A got along with next-door neighbor Musician B, whereas numerous other musicians would, soon after a first encounter, find a reason to stop performing with Musician B. The greater tolerance is easy to understand: well-known people, even if they are "strange bedfellows," can help resolve social anxiety.

Attentional Bias

Social anxiety can lead to exaggerated importance and hyperawareness of subtle cues that might be (mis)interpreted as being criticism. This is called "attentional bias," which can lead to a self-fulfilling prophecy. Returning to the aforementioned example, if Musician C had heard that Musician B was commonly negative towards others, Musician C would be primed with expectancy of disliking the Musician B, and the least negative thing that was said or done might be over weighted, thereby bringing about the self-fulfilling prophecy of disliking Musician B.

Loneliness

The *joie de vivre* derived from music does not inoculate musicians from the fact that everyone is vulnerable to experiencing loneliness. Loneliness is the precursor to potentially devastating depression.

In the context of interpersonal interactions, loneliness can be connected to social anxiety, and lead to unpleasant emotional and behavioral consequences. Being lonely is not the same as positive solitude or being alone for a good reason. To clarify, if a musician becomes isolated because of social anxiety and experiences depression, this is a negative, unhealthy pattern. It is much different than a musician's choosing to seek solace by holing up and playing or singing the blues (so to speak).

Negative Self-Attributions

Music performance and the concomitant interpersonal interactions are subject to the musician's self-attributions. Although unrealistically high self-regard is unhelpful, considering oneself to lack artistry or competency or to be unattractive and unworthy of acceptance by listeners or other musicians will open the door to negative conditions that will potentially be self-defeating.

Continuing with the earlier discussion of social anxiety, negative causal attributions to oneself lead to loneliness, which can progress to anxiety, frustration, and depression relevant to the interpersonal interactions inherent to musicianship. Becoming fixated on elusive musical success is self-defeating and can produce and eventuate in severe depression.

The musician who seems to be constantly lonely is wallowing in self-negativity. Both social anxiety and loneliness can be short lived (temporary) or long term (chronic). Often loneliness will be accompanied by self-blaming. Obviously this sort of mindset is unhealthy and counterproductive for musicianship and life in general, and may require help from a mental health professional.

Research supports that adolescents and young adults may be the loneliest age group. Since interest and commitment to music often surges in the middle and high school and college years, this principle is important for music education programs.

On a positive note, loneliness seems to decrease with maturity, although late in life, the age-related problems (health issues and death of friends and loved ones) may reintroduce loneliness. On the latter, one musician told how he found it disheartening that his physical health kept him from fulfilling his life-long ambition of "going on the road." A renowned trumpeter played full blast in his dying hours in the hospice. Another trumpeter was disheartened because his health precluded performing, saying "This is not how I want my music career and life to end" (note the equating of music and life). Numerous musicians in their later years have reported a near-obsession with practicing music, recognizing that it helped counteract age-related concerns.

For healthy musicianship, every musician should accept realistically that there is no guarantee of attaining noteworthy musical artistry, and recognize that there should be a constructive plan for improving musicianship (and one's lot in life) through study, practice, and adaptations to one's self-concept, such as via capitalizing on social relations. Having an overall constructive and healthy life style is essential for optimum musicianship.

Some musicians have reported bluntly that they believe that their music kept them alive and healthier than they would have been without the music. One of my former music students continued to practice and perform well into his nineties. Another musician, with all sorts of physical maladies, played constantly at home and with a big band until he, too, reached his nineties. He was quick to acknowledge that being around other musicians buoyed his spirits, and musical stimulation had a positive neurological impact. Numerous nonagenarian musicians attest that their commitment to music sharpened their minds (memory), which is supported by considerable and increasing empirical research.

Social skills are important for a positive life style. If conditions such as social anxiety lead the musician to experience loneliness or depression and become immersed in preoccupations about failure, there may well be a slippery slope into withdrawal from constructive social relationships, a pattern that can lead to self-destructive activities (such as alcohol and abuse of other substances).

Lonely people, who may commonly misperceive how others view them, can benefit from professional help. A competent mental health professional can help the musician realistically appraise social competence, cultivate skills for social interactions, and identify additional sources of positive reinforcement. Successful musicianship requires a conscious safety net against loneliness, depression, and self-destructive impulses and actions.

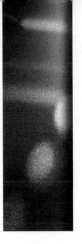

8

Musical Attachments

D ue to common usage, the terms "attachments" and "intimacy" may seem to be a bit out of place in a book about music and social relations. Not true. Musical attachments and intimacy may be neglected by some publications about musicianship, but they are not out of place.

By definition, attachment refers to having a sense of belonging and trust. In turn, the attachment system relies on intimacy, an extreme emotional closeness between two or more people (Fiske, 2004). This interpersonal state allows each person to enter into the personal space of the other person(s)—and here is an important point—without causing discomfort to that person. Each person gains detailed knowledge or in depth understanding of the other person(s), which can usually be characterized as involving closeness, familiarity, and affection, perhaps even love.

Let us take the example of the social relationship between a music performer and the audience. From various types of analyses, it seems clear that the performance is not, in a sense, complete without an emotional connection to the audience. Goodwin (1986) indicates that the performer and audience shape each other, particularly if there is overt participation in the interactive state (the performer and listener doing something together). The interpersonal interaction fosters an "intimate zone," the psychological distance or emotional scope adopted by those involved with the musical interaction. For example, in countless concerts, I have witnessed a surge of positivism between the musicians and audience when a sing-along or even hand clapping begins—there is interpersonal interaction.

Attachment Theory

When any sort of relationship is formed, expectations develop. With expectations comes an "attachment," an emotional bond that can be positive, negative, or mixed. By being "attached," the people become interdependent, with the type of bond influencing strongly how the relationship will evolve. Somewhat surprisingly, virtually any type of interpersonal attachment (such as might be formed between musicians in an ensemble) is almost preordained by the nature of the attachments experienced with caregivers during childhood. More will be said about this matter.

Attachment is an adaptive response, necessary for survival physically and emotionally. How one attaches to others is influenced by both genetics and caregiver-infant experiences. Aronson, Wilson, and Akert (2010) cite research studies that support: "a person's genotype may predispose him or her to a specific attachment style, which will then be further affected, one way or the other, by influence in the environment" and "it currently appears that one's genes account for 20 percent to 45 percent of the anxious and avoidant styles, with one's environment accounting for the rest" (p. 312).

If the caregiver-infant relationship created trust, the youngster is apt to grow up with no major concern about abandonment and will, instead, have a positive sense of self-worth. When the person expects to be liked or loved, a secure attachment style will develop. To the contrary, if the early caregiver-infant relationship suppressed attachment needs because intimacy was refused or rebuffed, it will be difficult for the infant or child to develop attachments later in life (i.e., there will be an avoidant attachment style). If the relationship with the caregiver led the infant or young child to be concerned that the caregiver would not respond positively to attempts at intimacy, there will likely be a high level of anxiety later on (in other words, there will be an anxious/ambivalent attachment style).

Yes, these types of attachment will continue to potentially influence social relationships throughout life. For example, a musician with secure attachment qualities is most apt to get along with other musicians and, in fact, communicate in a positive and effective manner with listeners. The same can be said about music educators connecting to their students in general, choral, and instrumental music. On the contrary, the insecure musician will lack self worth and be distrustful, characteristics that will likely lead to problematic social relations, whether in career or otherwise.

Why is attachment style important? By now, it should be obvious that it is influential, perhaps even determinative, of the musician's potential for developing intimacy. Why is intimacy important to musicianship? As indicated, intimacy creates the positive route in all musical aspects, including comfort with one's own musical efforts, interpersonal relationships (such as in an ensemble or teaching role), and communication to others to define the evaluation of one's musical endeavors.

Said simply, intimacy involves the musician's sharing information, relying on, and taking risks with another person. The bottom line is the people in an intimate relationship are concerned about the other's welfare and happiness, perhaps even more than they are concerned about their own preferences and needs.

It is important to realize that the aforementioned childhood experiences connected to attachment style are not 100% controlling in adulthood. Since the person, during the maturational process, experiences all sorts of other psychological influences, the attachment style brought forward from childhood is subject to modification, for better or for worse. Franzoi (2009) says: "It appears that people are most likely to undergo attachment style changes when they grapple with stressful, life-altering [positive or negative] events that expose them to experiences that challenge their existing attachment beliefs" (p. 387). This principle would suggest and justify, for example, that the effective music educator would purposefully use music to change students' lives. Indeed, I believe that the social and emotional aspects of music make it a powerful tool for remodeling attachment style.

When those in the world of music create intimacy and engage in social relations, those in the exchange become merged psychologically. This leads each person to adjust his or her attributions about the other(s) to infer similarity. It is human nature to search for similarities with others with whom there will be contact. Evolutionary psychologists believe this effort is fueled by the arcane notion that if someone is like us, there is less apt to be a preset that the person is an enemy (in other words, an intimate relationship poses limited or no threat, such as to obtaining "musical success").

Once the bond is in place, resources are blended as well, as exemplified by musicians exchanging mouthpieces, giving away a woodwind reed or a guitar pick without promise of payment, doing things for each other, and so on. In other words, there is willingness for social exchange, such as allowing resources to flow back and forth without awareness or concern for any possible rewards and costs.

Obviously, the lack of positive qualities such as caring, understanding, and sharing can lead to a decrease in intimacy (e.g., less trust). If one musician in an ensemble is "stand-offish" when it comes to niceties in the relationship, it will seem like distrust and social distancing, and the potential for developing intimacy will decrease. Note that, since "attacking" an opponent requires use of resources and involves risks, encounters with distant or difficult musicians can often be handled best by a "live and let live" attitude, with no remorse, guilt, or other negativity invested in the lack of a positive relationship with the person.

A transactive memory system is a powerful unifying force in an intimate relationship. Stated differently, people in an intimate relationship have a shared memory system, which allows one to benefit from the information remembered by another, that is, "a system in which information to be remembered is distributed among various members of a group, who can then each be relied on to provide the information when it is needed" (VandenBos, 2007, p. 951). It allows the members of a relationship to have, in a sense, responsibility for different types of information that can be drawn upon to make shared efforts better. In a jazz group, for example, one person may be expected to remember the key for a tune, another may have the unspoken role of primary innovator in improvisation, while another may accept the responsibility of remembering how to get the "blankety-blank sound system to work right." The transactive memory system between musicians potentially leads to an improved attachment style in music-based intimate relationships.

Friendship

Although everyone is unique in the elements of the need for friendship, human nature, as mentioned earlier, leads to efforts (conscious or unconscious) to find similarity and create positive relationships. Thus, unless there is some significant character problem with a person, musicians coming together should move toward friendship.

Between two or more people, a friendship is relatively long lasting. In addition to wanting to gain satisfaction or fulfillment of one's own needs, each friend tends to be concerned about meeting the other friend's needs and interests as well.

A friendship commonly evolves from shared experiences that produced mutual benefits and gratifications. Also, there is likely to be interpersonal social and emotional support. For example, I have several friends from my musical days fifty years ago, with whom I still have (nonmusical) contact and know that we offer each other interpersonal social and emotional support (such as being concerned about health and well being). Of course we also share a positive transactive memory system, which can yield positive effects musically. For example, reminiscing with a long-ago musician about when I once played a now-neglected instrument led me to reactive my practicing on it.

A friendship leads to the people revealing personal and intimate qualities to each other (that is, self-disclosure), perhaps things that would not be revealed readily to mere acquaintances or maybe even to oneself. Personal characteristics enter into this process. For example, I am somewhat prone to not tell others about things that I consider to be highly personal, but I have several musician (and nonmusician) friends who all too readily engage in "too much information" that is really not relevant to our friendship.

The more intimate and longer the friendship, the more likely it is that there will be increasing (more sensitive) self-disclosure. Said differently, social penetration theory holds that self-disclosures in an established relationship increase intimacy. However, if the relationship turns sour (e.g., one person disappoints or hurts the other), there may be disengagement and depenetration. As example, among my long-term musician friends, I had a highly positive social relationship with Musician A (based to a large extent on our earlier musical years together). However, when it became evident that Musician A was not trustworthy in business, which offended my value system, I stopped all communications with him, albeit that he and I have no open animosity towards each other.

Social Networking Between Musicians

On one of my social network affiliations, I have an extensive list of musicians. Although some of the musicians resort to posts that are rather mundane and unrelated to music per se, I make it a point to emphasize musical information, as do the majority of people on my list of "friends" (I remove those who overdo pictures of their pets and talk about politics, religion, or ailments).

Do those of us on the list have bona fide social relations? In a sense, the answer is "yes," namely because of the positive tone to the communications about our shared musical interests. In another sense, the answer is "no," because we have information about only a minor part of each other's life. And, with rare exceptions, there is no face-to-face contact, and no performing music together.

Virtual meetings (via the internet, cell phones, or other electronic means) are unique in some ways, but have certain conditions that would be present in face-to-face meetings. For example, in accord with social penetration theory, which emphasizes increasing self-disclosure in a relationship, the more two people interact, say, by e-mail or texting, the more personal and intimate information is increasingly revealed.

Although research is lacking, it may be that a goodly portion of the people who rely on computer-mediated social relationships find it difficult to form positive social relationships in the real world. Electronic self-presentation is subject to gross distortions or falsehoods. For example, on the electronic social networks, a substantial number of people post an attractive photograph, often from years gone by or enhanced by computer software. Also, instead of candidly presenting information that reveals the actual self, there is a tendency to present the ideal self. For example, I have found a tendency among musicians to foster an impression of playing better, performing more often, and having greater celebrity than their eventual electronic admissions would support.

The psychological principle of social penetration should be a cold reminder to be cautious and to not believe everything that is posted on a social network. The following could be a mantra: discussion of superficial topics progresses to more intimate exchanges, which creates personal vulnerability.

Ignoring Negatives in Favor of Positives

Social psychology research supports that, in a new relationship, there is a tendency to wear "rose-colored glasses." Much like the early stage of a romantic relationship, when musicians join together (such as to form a band), they may be sifting out the negative and emphasizing best qualities and perhaps even thinking the compatibility is better than is true (that is, there is aggrandizement). Recall the rock group that I described as being obsessed with their big break-out night and upon disappointment, immediately disbanded.

Just as initial passion changes through familiarity in a romance (when passion wanes, it is commonly replaced by companionship), a musical affiliation becomes more reality-based. If romantic partners or musical associates have strong self-concepts, they are, even with the onset of realistic awareness, more apt to view each other's flaws or limitations in the best possible light. Thus, if a commercial ensemble does stay together, it is likely that the members may have healthier self-concepts involved. Although there are countless examples, Diamond Rio (Diamond Rio & Roland, 2009) and the Statler Brothers (Reid & Reid, 2007) come to mind as long-lasting ensembles that seem to have made positive adaptations. Incidentally, it is my opinion that the musical genre is not determinative of the notion that well-defined self-concepts contribute to survival of a group.

A member of a performing group that had been together for decades said that the survival was probably due, to a large extent, to the fact that all of the members got over problems quickly. This comment would suggest that, even when disdain occurred, each musician returned to awareness, consciously or unconsciously, of the others' positive qualities, such as the benefits derived from the shared efforts.

Certainly success can shape the survival of an ensemble as well. For example, the long-term success of various chamber music groups, the Beatles, and Peter, Paul, and Mary add credence to this idea.

Will Musical Bonding Endure?

A friend of mine often says, "nothing is forever." During a lifetime, this may or may not be true about the social relations that lead to musical bonding.

As described numerous places in this book, a musical relationship is, to be sure, vulnerable to dissolution, much like any relationship, friendship, or even a marriage. The "divorce" can be either formally by law (de jure) or informally by abandonment (de facto).

With musical associations, such as between the founding members of an ensemble, emotional ties may weaken and there may be replacements or disbanding. As mentioned in the context of a failure to achieve a shared aspiration for musical success, the aftermath may be negative, unfortunate, and hostile. There have been countless lawsuits between former band members over some disputed right (such as who owns the name of the band or financial remuneration owed). As with a divorce between a husband and wife, one is left to wonder what attracted and bonded them in the earlier days?

Again, like a marriage, a musical group may have others influencing their continued existence, such as negative views being expressed by family members, friends, listeners, audiences, management, and others (for example, society at large). The potential for disapproval and discrimination often produces a negative impact on commitment to the musical relationship.

Staying with the marriage metaphor, the happiest union involves spouses who attend to and fulfill each other's array of needs. Likewise with a musical group, relationship maintenance behaviors involve caring and sharing resources, affection, and self-disclosure.

Be it a domestic or musical bonding, social exchange theory considers the ratio of rewards and costs inherent to the relationship. Inequity may damage romantic relationships (albeit that the evaluation of the rewards and costs is highly subjective and may not be based in reality). For example, if one musician receives greater accolades than the other musicians in an ensemble, human inclination would be for that member to want "top billing" and a greater share of the rewards. Of course, there are formulas that astute attorneys and accountants can apply to assure that each member's receipts are compatible with his or her contribution to the musical enterprise. However, it is not unusual for personal egotism to enter the picture, with a denial of mathematical reasoning or contractual terms and conditions.

It would be tempting to assert that low self-esteem leads to an inability to devote fully to a shared musical project (or a marriage). However, research contradicts that idea; high self-esteem is not a prerequisite for commitment to another person (Franzoi, 2009). There should be, of course, caution against overgeneralization of research.

Whether high or low self-esteem, a person may find intimacy difficult. As discussed earlier, the linchpin may be the presence or absence of secure attachment styles. If the person has stable and sufficiently strong self-respect AND a secure attachment style, the person is most apt to be capable of expression and acceptance of intimacy, as well as handling relationship conflict in a constructive manner. The musician who hopes to have enduring musical bonding would be wise to aspire to this personal model.

Satisfying intimate relationships benefit from harboring positive evaluations of each other, even if they are illusions. This is called partner-enhancing bias; by being positive, a self-fulfilling prophecy may be created. Therefore, if Musician A harbors a positive impression of Musician B (such as expecting impressive improvisation), there will be a tendency to search for and recognize creativity and overlook unimpressive musical performance.

Similarly, being able to convey empathic recognition and sensitivity to each other's thoughts and feelings promotes satisfaction in the musical relationship. Empathy involves accepting the other person's frame of mind and vicariously experiencing the other's feelings, perceptions, and thoughts. Not surprising, giving each other social support through information and emotions improves conditions in the relationship. Regrettably, being empathic is not always easily gained. Although a person can cultivate empathy, there is considerable variation between people in their empathic capabilities.

Remember the old song, "You always hurt the one you love, the one you shouldn't hurt at all?" Research reveals that married people tend to be more critical of each other than would be justified, and the same response can occur between musicians. It is likely that the nature of intimate musical relationships means that a certain amount of hurt is inevitable.

Research suggests that perpetrators of negative actions seek to redefine and justify it, trying to dissociate from being responsible for something wrongful. They may, for example, describe the situation in an unrealistically positive manner and reject the idea that the action was significantly harmful to the relationship. Among musicians trying to justify rejection of a colleague, there may fault finding and exaggeration of the person's limitations or shortcomings (I have witnessed numerous rejections of musicians because of unlikable personal characteristics, not because of musical factors).

Given the importance of musical relationships for self-esteem, it is not surprising that the dissolution or termination of a musical bond leads to stress and emotional distress, especially for the person who did not initiate the breakup. From research, there is reason to believe that the person who initiates the breakup experiences less distress. Although the breakup of a musical group is often shrouded in secrecy to avoid legal liability, there have been numerous musical scenarios that would seemingly reflect that those who stayed with the group did not suffer the pangs of remorse as much as the one(s) who departed. There may be some intense and bittersweet feelings when, after a period of time without the member who was booted out (and perhaps with a waning of success), the ensemble realizes the benefits of the person and "sweet talks" him or her into rejoining the group.

To wrap up this discussion positively, research indicates that negative events, such as the breakup of an ensemble, can promote personal growth. Granted, when the person is immersed in loneliness, sadness, anger, and depression and experiences a sense of rejection, the potential for positive growth may provide little consolation—but hope springs eternal. For an ejected musician, it might prove to be an opportunity to develop a solo career that would not have otherwise occurred.

9

The Lasting Ensemble

The high school years involve all sorts of possible group affiliations, such as sports teams, cheerleading, chorus, band, and science and other clubs. Being in a high school or college chorus, band, or orchestra (I will combine the two groups into the term "bandies") allows a student to fulfill social and affiliation needs, receive positive reinforcement from other students and the experience (applause at a concert), and refine the musical self-concept.

To this day, I get clear images of my participation in musical ensembles, especially as an undergraduate music major in college. I am not alone.

It is common for a community to have a chorus, concert band, or orchestra for everyday folks. In this sort of ensemble, there is a common denominator: the participants are engaging in "age regression." When I played with a community wind symphony, many (most?) of the musicians were into their middle or later years; their instrument cases often had high school and college decals that revealed youthful participation in some musical group and there was a propensity for the members to talk about those early musical experiences.

For most students who participate in a musical group in high school or college, the musical self-concept will be set aside for a career in some non-musical endeavor. Regardless, through the passing years, the emotional passion connected to being a "bandie" often continues and becomes an idealized aspiration across the life span.

A sedate senior female was devoted to her religious ministry, but would only reluctantly skip a practice with a community band in order to attend some church activity. To the surprise of her parishioners, she adopted the name "Brassy Lady" to indicate her commitment to her instrument.

After forty-plus years as a highly successful professor (with leadership in his profession at the national level), a fellow retired from the academy and promptly joined four community ensembles. He reported, "All of the years that I labored in the university, I longed for the days when I was in the high school and college bands—now I spend three, sometimes four, nights a week in rehearsals and I love it."

A retired classroom teacher said, "The Christmas season is always special for me because our community choir sings the Messiah." She went on to say, "By the end of the year, everyone who joined in the fall seems like part of the musical family."

Countless younger musicians find relief from the pursuit of a "day job" career by being in an ensemble. I know of several groups made up of musicians from law, medicine, or some other high-stress professions. Regardless of age, the underlying dimension is the same: musical affiliations are extremely (incomparably?) rewarding, enhanced by the emotional passion, creativity, and self-esteem that are obtained.

Further, it is not just adults who sense being enveloped by music. The reason that music education is so popular with elementary, middle, and high school students is exactly the same.

Group Principles for an Ensemble

Because of my professorial "day job," I had the unique experience of studying group psychotherapy at the Washington School of Psychiatry for a couple years. We read materials on theory and research, heard lectures, attended seminars, watched from behind a one-way mirror as seasoned professionals conducted therapy with groups, and conducted groups ourselves. I learned that the group context has the potential to offer personal benefits that might not occur in a non-group context. Being a musician, I easily transferred the group-related learning to my sitting in my practice room playing music alone, which was enjoyable, but there was much more to be gained by participating in a musical ensemble.

Defining a Group

A group involves two or more people who become dependent on each other, especially for completing a task at the best quality possible. There are emotional ties and contacts that are frequent enough to preserve the recognized connections between the group members. These qualities are fully applicable to defining any kind of musical ensemble.

Because of the wish for self-enhancement, it is human nature to want to be associated with people who will add positively to one's social identity. Thus, if there is a musical ensemble available to a musician, the person will consider whether membership will bring about positives or negatives to oneself.

One musician reported declining repeated requests to participate in a community ensemble because "several of the old-timers and the conductor have been described as bossy." If an ensemble acquires a negative reputation, social psychology indicates that members or potential members will distance or avoid an affiliation to cutoff reflected failure. This is similar to how the self-concept evaluates whether another person will bring positive or negative conditions into a social relationship.

Ingroup versus Outgroup

With a group of any kind, the tendency is to want members who will contribute positively. That is, there is a wish to build solidarity through similarities and mutual benefits, thereby creating strong ingroup identification. If a person does not contribute or cannot justify acceptance, he or she will be relegated to outgroup status.

The positive bonding together of the group members reflects social cohesiveness or "groupiness." Cohesion is potentially influenced by group size, member similarity, and diversity. For the musical self-concept, one's social identity depends on ingroup contacts.

Now for a problem that music groups face. Research indicates that, when a group (like a musical ensemble) has strong cohesion (closeness), their view of others may become unrealistic, tainted, or defensive. There is "ingroup bias." This is a tendency for the group to glorify ingroup members, such as by giving favorable evaluations and rewards, which are not available to outgroup members.

A blues musician described how a handful of musicians playing in the same venues had "become my family, and just like families, we all have different personalities and love and hate each other at times, but there is a special bond." And here is his statement relevant to ingroup bias: "Sometimes outsiders are welcomed into the family, but no matter what their playing abilities, if their personalities don't mesh . . . they don't get to hang with us very long." The question remains, do these ingroup blues musicians see and hear the new kids on the block objectively or is there some sort of ingroup bias? Before the question can be answered, there are more social psychology principles to be considered.

Size Matters

True to group theory, the ideal size of an ensemble for a particular musician will depend on the need for affiliation and cognitive ability to process information about the costs and benefits of membership with the particular group. A larger group is, logically, more difficult for an individual musician to influence or control; even a small group of members may find that they have much less impact on a larger group than they think is deserved. Said differently, such as with the previously described blues group, any individual's motivation that is selfish or not reinforcing of the total group might not be powerful or even acceptable. Taken to excess, self-serving can, of course, lead to expulsion of even an ingroup member.

One highly capable musician admitted that he avoided larger ensembles because "I don't get a chance to be heard." However, several smaller ensembles rejected him because "he constantly wants the limelight." He was essentially limited to an ensemble for which he was the leader from the outset.

Similarity and Diversity

As for similarity and diversity, ingroup members tend to be more similar than different, and strive to encourage shared responsibility and interpersonal compatibility through emphasizing their similarities. Therefore, in a musical ensemble, shared interests and psychological need fulfillment provide members with the incentive to contribute to the development and maintenance of a cohesive group.

Diversity in personal characteristics among group members is not all bad. In a musical ensemble, having different kinds of people can improve problem solving, meeting goals, and creativity. Certainly with musical creativity, having members with different interests and competencies can be potential positives.

For example, in one commercial ensemble, the leader makes it a point to include musicians with significantly different musical interests and skills. The selection process is not limited to one gender or age group. This process exemplifies how diversity can multiply and enrich resources.

As a related example of diversity, I once booked about a dozen elementary and middle school concerts. Since the music was essentially Dixieland and there was to be a music education objective, I was pleased when an attractive college-aged female agreed to be our tuba player; her appearance and full-sized tuba clearly won special approval from the students (and for the girls, she had a particular social modeling effect).

Another benefit from diversity within a musical ensemble is that an individual member can gain in self-verification from comparing his or her musical characteristics or qualities to those of other group members who have different characteristics or qualities. For example, one jazz group has an age span of about 30 to 75—just the difference in stage of life positively influences all of the members in the group (such as for preferred tunes, improvisation, and energy level). The diversity also broadens audience appeal.

Being a Team Player

Being a team player seems to be part of the American way. This does not mean that the individual always puts the group ahead of his or her own needs, but there is a reasonable degree of emotional commitment to the group that will yield benefits to both the member and the group as a whole (and consequently for the other members of the group).

In a musical ensemble, attempts to subvert or lessen group cohesion will trigger negative reactions. A group has a limited degree of tolerance for objections from or protests by a group member. Said differently, a grumpy, uncooperative musician will not be welcomed for very long.

The Purpose of an Ensemble

The primary purpose of a musical ensemble is easy to identify: produce excellent music. But there are other secondary purposes as well.

A group seeks to satisfy the members' socioemotional or affiliation needs and to accomplish instrumental (purposeful) tasks. Task-oriented groups are strongly committed to production, as will bring about rewards, payoffs, benefits, etc. At the same time, groups serve to provide the members with good feelings, such as a sense of self-worth, fulfilling a need to be social or affiliate with others, and so on. Certainly all of these purposes are appropriate for a musical ensemble.

The Structure of an Ensemble

An ensemble functions within a structure, which is supposedly determined by how many musicians are to be involved and what vocal parts or instruments would seemingly be preferred. Of course, depending on the nature of the group, pragmatics will be important; for example, there may be a shortage of the preferred kind of musicians (e.g., those who play a particular instrument or can sing a harmony part).

An ensemble's structure develops and is maintained in an evolutionary manner. That is, the ensemble identifies its purposes, goals, and objectives and establishes rules, communication channels, and roles (both for participants in general and for the leaders in specific). In other words, the structure prescribes and proscribes who does what, when, and how.

The structure of an ensemble also has social norms, social roles, and status systems. Social norms are the expected standards of behavior and beliefs, social roles are the expectations that members in a given situation are to fulfill, and the status system is the distribution of power among the group members. Note that the notion of equality is seldom factual. In the context of an ensemble, it is common for some musicians to be more "equal" than others because of leadership, longevity, skill, or whatever.

Five Phases of Ensemble Membership

When I first became immersed in group theory, I was impressed with how the seasoned instructors could predict, with surprising accuracy, what would happen in the next group session. The predictions might be about the group as a whole or about given members in the group. In the subsequent years, I have learned that reasonably accurate judgments can be made about expected changes within a group. Based on information from observational analyses, the functions of any group (such as a musical ensemble) can be predicted with a surprising degree of accuracy.

Social psychology research supports a group and its members will progress through five phases. For exemplary purposes, let's use the blues group that was described earlier.

The Investigative Phase: A new musician arrives in the neighborhood (so to speak), and looks at what is happening (reconnoitering). In the investigative phase, the musician seeks introductions and a chance to play with established ensembles. There will be a reciprocal commitment that develops between certain musicians.

The Socialization Phase: After joining the ensemble, the new member engages in socialization within the group. There interactions give the band members an opportunity to shape the new musician's thinking and behavior.

The Maintenance Phase: When the new musician has become well entrenched as a band member, the person is deemed to be a full member and contributor to the maintenance of the group as roles and goals are pursued. The ensemble has now been restructured to accommodate the new member. This is when specialized roles may be defined or old roles may be altered or redefined (such as who will play lead on or what will be the key for a particular tune, which saxophone should be used, etc.).

The Resocialization Phase: If any ensemble member, new or old, becomes marginal to the group, continued membership may require additional relationship building or resocialization. There will be attempts to foster acceptable role expectations and mutually agreed upon compromises of differences.

The Remembrance Phase: Once a member has left the group or the group has terminated, the remembrance phase arrives, hopefully offering "sweet memories" that will have positive influence in the future (after the death of one ensemble leader, comments were often made about "it's just not the same without [so-and-so]").

Neither an ensemble member nor the group must absolutely pass from one phase to the next. There can be regression and movement back and forth. The changes and phases will not necessarily be in a predictable sequence. Yes, even the most astute and insightful musician with considerable experience and training may not always be able to predict group or individual behavior or dynamics accurately all of the time.

Ensemble Influence on Individual Behavior

As with membership in any social group, joining a musical ensemble subjects the person to influence from others. The influence comes potentially from each ensemble member, as well as from any cliques, the formal and informal leadership, and the group as a whole.

Social Facilitation

The mere presence of another person can influence a person's behavior, such as motivating an ensemble member to learn and to sing or play better. This is known as the social facilitation effect. However, there is also the possibility that the presence of and scrutiny from others can lead a musician to be inhibited, intimidated, and less able to perform.

The social facilitation principle derived from the research of social psychologist Robert Boleslaw Zajonc [1923–2008]. To summarize social facilitation: "What this means is that the presence of others will enhance correct execution of well-learned tasks at the same time that it will interfere with or inhibit correct performance of novel, unlearned tasks" (Franzoi, 2009, p. 304). In other words, social facilitation means that the presence of others can bring out the best in someone. I have heard numerous musicians mention, "When I am in an ensemble, I usually play better than when I am practicing at home." For some musicians, having others present can lead to sharp focus and, consequently, an improved performance.

In the context of a musical ensemble, it is easy to recognize how any musician is potentially vulnerable to the social facilitation principle. As mentioned, not only can a fellow musician (say the conductor or first chair of the section) have a special influence, a combination of others (say the "officers" of a community choir, band, or orchestra) can, with varying degrees of authority, send out influential messages. Likewise, given the reputation of the group (say a renowned jazz band or a symphony), all members impose an influence that requires accommodation, adherence, and satisfaction in order for a particular musician to retain membership.

Evaluation Apprehension

As I have discussed in several places, including in the section on the "Naked Musician," music performance involves exposure of one's personal qualities. Baring one's musicianship, the musician then, like everyone in a social encounter, engages in conscious or unconscious self-evaluation, that is, considers what others are likely thinking about the musician.

Obviously being a member of an ensemble means that there is always one or more others who are aware (presumably) of what each musician is doing. Just having someone else present in a rehearsal or concert may increase evaluation apprehension. The musician may experience uneasiness or worry due to the desire to be evaluated favorably by the fellow musicians, as well as any listeners (audience). Evaluation apprehension may be more powerful than being distracted by the presence of other people.

Social Loafing

If a member believes that others are not monitoring or interested in what goes on in the group, there may be a slacking off or reduction of effort; this is, called social loafing. Many musicians have told about feeling safe in an ensemble "because when I flub a note, no one will hear it" (of course the musician hears it, which impacts on self-evaluation). Since being judged individually can sometimes be avoided in an ensemble, social loafing allows the musician to reduce effort and be less stressed.

At a performance of a community swing band, the director kept saying, "Listen to yourself and to the others too." As amateurs, the musicians seemed minimally focused on the quality of their individual performance (there was even "clowning around") and lacked concern about creating a unified ensemble sound. There was certainly social loafing.

A musical ensemble allows the musicians to experience a diffusion of responsibility. By avoiding being judged individually, the musician is apt to feel less responsible for the musical outcome. The downside, however, is that the musician cannot justly experience pride in a fine performance, although some personality structures would allow the person to take credit, even though credit is not truly due.

Good musicianship does not support social loafing. If members of a musical ensemble detect social loafing, ostracism may be applied.

Highly competent members of the ensemble may increase their efforts to counteract the likelihood that some other members who will perform poorly. For example, iconic jazz cornetist, pianist, and composer, Leon Bismark "Bix" Beiderbeck [1903–1931] purposefully and commonly "carried" the bands with which he played (Lion, 2007). In keeping with the psychology of leadership, a musician with the charisma attributed to Beiderbeck could certainly help accomplish that purpose.

Rising to the Challenge

Biographical accounts support that Beiderbeck and countless others like him could/can, in fact, inspire, guide, and teach less able musicians to elevate their musicianship. This is one aspect for seating musicians by ability in a concert band or orchestra.

In opposition to social loafing, less competent members of the group may be highly motivated when the group success depends on them, as opposed to situations where they are performing for only their own benefit. In order to retain social acceptance, ensemble membership can bring out the best in the musicians.

Decision Making in Ensembles

Among musicians, the decision-making that occurs in ensembles is a frequent target of derision. Too often, because of character deficits (such as an faulty self-concept, narcissism, and impulsiveness), the leader, conductor, or "power structure" will use the decision-making process ineptly. In one troubled community ensemble, a would-be leader declared, "I don't care what the rest of you prefer, I am the President and will make the decisions."

Ideally, every member of a musical ensemble should be involved to some degree in decision-making, such as the selection of compositions or tunes for performance. Of course there are some scenarios where a particular source, such as the musical director, conductor, or coterie of section chairs, are expected to assume responsibility and make the final decisions. Nonetheless, consensus building and tact are prerequisites for successful leadership.

Decision-Making Stages

When a decision is to be made, the decision-makers need to receive relevant and authoritative information (orientation), and then move on to the discussion, decision, and implementation stages. At each stage, there will be various types of social influence, which will be determined, to some degree, by the ensemble's context and structural/operational issues that are relevant to the decision-making.

The astute decision-maker will be cognizant that the initial attitudes and opinions expressed by the musicians may involve enhancement or exaggeration, and that there is a risk of warring between members (group polarization).

In the early stage(s) of decision-making, there may be a tendency to take illogical or unnecessary risks (trying to play a composition that is well beyond the ability of most of the musicians). Of course the decision-making could go in the opposite direction, resulting in being too conservative (performing overly simplistic music). Overly conservative decisions may be connected to the self-concept qualities of the musicians who make the decision.

The basic idea is that, by being in a group context, the musicians are subtly and gradually reinforced to shift attitudes to a more extreme point, be it more difficult or simple than is best. There is mutual persuasion, with a gradual lessening on concern about self- or ensemble-evaluation to arrive at the correct or best solution.

Group Polarization

Group polarization is more apt to occur in discussions about important issues, as opposed to issues of minimal importance. Meta-analysis research supports two viewpoints: (1) issues involving judgmental tasks with no objectively right or wrong solutions will rely most heavily on a comparison of views held by group members to the views held by others; and (2) if the issue involves intellectual tasks, group members rely most on the information presented in arguments. The former principle refers to social comparison, the latter is called persuasive argumentation.

In a symphony orchestra, the musicians urged management to play more compositions that would be known to audience members. On the contrary, the management doggedly pursued "education the community to fine, classical music." Clearly there is no objectively right or wrong decision, and musicians and management alike should set forth a meaningful rationale for any preference or determination.

Groupthink

Groupthink is a provocative concept in social psychology. It refers to a "deterioration of mental efficiency, reality testing, and moral judgment in a group that results from an excessive desire to reach consensus" (Franzoi, 2009, p. 319). Due to the important role played by the musical self-concept possessed by each ensemble member, the inherent deficits (insecurity, obsession with proving artistry or gaining success) can result in serious negative effects for a group.

As said above, the unique and integral role of each musician's self-concept may, regrettably, make ensembles particularly vulnerable to groupthink. In my professional activities, I have witnessed groupthink in all types of musical ensembles, cutting across all genres, contexts, and levels of musicianship—all because of faulty self-concepts among those in the ensemble. Consequently, I tend to believe that any ensemble has the potential to resort to groupthink, notwithstanding its obvious negative outcomes.

For groupthink in a musical ensemble, the threshold issue is that the group wants everyone to be in accord with each other. That is, the motivation is for consensus in the ensemble (so far, this is an honorable objective). Unfortunately, if consensus is overdone, with resulting lapses in efficiency, reality testing, and moral judgment, there will be negative effects.

Yale University psychology professor Irving Janis [1918–1990] posited that two factors, a threatening situational context and structural and procedural faults, create a pathway to groupthink. In other words, if a group is not effectively achieving its goals and the membership has deficits (e.g., character disorders, limited intellect, poor coping skills, faulty self-concepts, inadequate musicianship), an ill-advised framework of groupthink may be adopted.

Groupthink will be reflected in three symptoms: an overestimation of quality for one's ingroup, close-mindedness, and increased conformity pressure. Numerous historical decisions, such as in government, reveal significantly more groupthink characteristics than occur in successful decisions. With decision-making in musical ensemble, groupthink can lead to disastrous consequences.

From information in a music law seminar for attorneys that I attended (and other sources), I conclude there is reason to believe that symphonies are particularly vulnerable to groupthink, be it within management or the musicians' association. However, no musical genre or type of ensemble is immune from groupthink.

For example, a hypothetical community concert band administration (the conductor and "officers") wants to increase its performance of classical music and lessen its use of tunes from modern-day Broadway musicals. Regardless, the majority of the musicians are dead set against the idea. As it turns out, the musicians are just everyday folks who have retrieved their high school or college instruments from the closet, are seldom taking music lessons, and do not have time (because of their "day jobs") to practice.

Moreover, those in the administration are viewed as bossy and self-absorbed. An "us-against-them" situation emerges.

Continuing with the example, in the administrative meetings, any contrary views from the musicians are discounted, any advocacy of modern-day musicals is criticized (with clear emotions), and there are repeated self-aggrandizing comments (righteousness). Devastating groupthink effects on morale, motivation, commitment, and musicianship are inevitable.

Now go back through the foregoing scenario and, still considering the choice of music to be played, substitute a symphonic board of directors for the community band administrators' and replace a symphony union-based bargaining team for the members of the community band. Or assume that it is a school music education program that pits the school administrator and teachers against the parents of the school musicians. I believe that no group, certainly not in the realm of music, is shielded from detrimental groupthink. The result can be expulsion of those who do not comply with the expectations and demands of those with power or disintegration of the ensemble.

Ensemble Leadership

Through research on leadership, social psychology has made important contributions to human resources, organizations, and productivity. In any group, a leader is one who exerts more influence, provides direction, and generates energy for others.

To build a strong musical ensemble, the group structure should support that any musician potentially be eligible to serve as some sort of leader, and it should be made clear that, if the role is accepted, it portends to be both rewarding and demanding (Northouse, 2009). In responding to an opportunity to be a leader among musicians, consideration should be given to the components of both the self-concept that is needed from social relationships (that is, does leadership fulfill psychological needs for the person) and musicianship (personal characteristics, competency, talent, communication, charisma, and so on).

Ethical Considerations

Social psychology supports that leadership of any kind, including among musicians, carries ethical responsibility: "Ethics is at the heart of leadership. When we assume the benefits of leadership, we also assume ethical burdens. I believe that we must make every effort to act in such a way as to benefit rather than damage others, to cast light instead of shadow" (Johnson, 2009, p. xvi).

Leadership among musicians requires a commitment to do the right thing. Whether a designated leader or not, every musician should adopt a goal of helping other musicians accomplish their self-fulfillment, personal aspirations, and musicianship.

Self-aggrandizement through attempts at leadership of others is not honorable. Too many would-be leaders have ended in disgrace because they pursued fulfilling their own needs, such as narcissistic self-adulation and financial enrichment, instead of focusing on benefiting others.

Task and Socioemotional Leadership

At one point in the past, leaders were thought to engage in (1) task leadership (accomplishing musical goals for the ensemble) and (2) socioemotional leadership (contributing positively to the emotional and interpersonal aspects of the members of the ensemble). Task-oriented leaders tend to be directive, whereas socioemotionally-oriented leaders are more democratic and convey positive messages and create supportive relationships. Although these two conditions are not considered fully determinative of successful leadership, they are still relevant and material.

Transformational Leadership

A more modern viewpoint is that the psychological aspects of charisma (that is, a personal quality that arouses popular loyalty and enthusiasm) contribute to transformational leadership that helps improve others' outlook and behavior for better performance by all concerned. Certainly in musicianship, this stance would be useful.

Transformational leaders should have a charismatic communication style. They inspire and create a vision (with some degree of specificity) for future success. For music ensembles, the leader(s) should strive to communicate an outlook for an improved state of affairs for the ensemble as a whole and each musician therein, and implement strategies that will move everyone toward achieving the musical vision.

Situation Control by an Open System

In organizational theory, an open system involves unfettered communications and potential input to decision-making for every person in the group. Further, within the contingency model of leadership, an open system also considers both task oriented and relationship oriented factors, as well as the degree to which the leader has situational control (Chance & Chance, 2002).

No one style is essential for effectiveness. Rather it depends on the situation. Situational control depends on the personal relationships involving the leader and members of the group, the leader's ability to influence the definition of goals and tasks, and how the group distributes power and authority, including to the recognized leader.

Leadership seems to be best demonstrated when there is an "open system," that is, a structure that has interdependent parts and values and considers new information from diverse sources. In simple terms, with a music ensemble of any kind, every musician should believe that his or her voice (opinion) is being considered by the leader(s). As is obvious in any rehearsal of a musical ensemble, the leader's style has a strong influence.

Avoiding a Social Dilemma

Throughout this chapter, there has been emphasis on the musical ensemble as a whole gaining benefits from its members. Of course, each musician presumably also receives benefits from being in the ensemble; otherwise he or she would likely drop out of (disassociate from) the group. The interests of the ensemble and the individual member (or subgroup of members) are not always in accord.

There will be instances when a particular musician (or subgroup) will act a certain way, perhaps for self-gain, that will produce a detrimental effect for the group. This kind of incident constitutes a social dilemma. There are five strategies for avoiding the negative effects of social dilemmas: "(1) establishing guidelines and sanctions against self-serving behavior, (2) getting people to understand how their actions help and hurt everyone's long-term welfare, (3) encouraging people to develop a group identity, (4) fostering the internalization of social values that encourage cooperation rather than competition, and (5) promoting group discussion that leads to cooperation commitments" (Franzoi, 2009, p. 330). These strategies will buttress the efforts by ensemble leaders to deal effectively with social dilemmas.

Ensemble members who contribute to a social dilemma will likely have mixed motives. They want what they can get from being selfish, but know that in the long run they will lose, such as being expelled from the ensemble or getting less from the other musicians.

With all that has been said about group members, there is no doubt that being identified with an ensemble can offer a great deal to an individual musician. The sense of "community" (being part of an organized whole) contributes to feelings of the self-identity and self-worth derived from being a musician.

Think about people who attend high school reunions. Sure there are memories of the "good old days when I was younger," but there is also a sense of being united with the former classmates. Incidentally, having attended a number of reunions, I am bemused at how the "bandies" tend to congregate. Of course, some colleges and universities now schedule annual reunion activities just for those who participated in musical ensembles.

10

Moving Toward Complete Musicianship

Much like a musical score, this chapter reflects and integrates major ideas about musicianship. However, it goes further. It gives emphasis to the psychological fuel that comes from music overall: emotions. It explains comprehensive musicianship as unifying the seven sectors of listening, learning (including analysis of the musical elements), practicing, teaching, arranging, composing, and performing. It addresses the question of whether comprehensive musicianship is determined by achieving (or at least seeking) excellence in all seven sectors of musicianship or from sensing fulfillment from accomplishments in just some of the sectors. To answer this complex question, consideration will be given to the role of informal (vernacular) versus formal musicianship, the need for individuation, the impact of music abilities on human development, music and body-mind health, effective interpersonal relations for musicianship, and the contribution made by improvisation.

Emotions and Music

At the risk of sounding like a cliché, music is the sound of emotion. As will be discussed, emotions can be positive or negative and are connected with a given pattern of physiological activity. Early on, psychologists recognized that emotions were complex, involving not only physiological processes, but also situational, cognitive, behavioral, and emotional responses, much of which is mediated neurologically (Shiraev, 2011).

There has been considerable research on the theoretical bases for emotions; and as might be expected, there are contradictory viewpoints. For the purpose of understanding musicianship, it is sufficient to rely on the so-called James-Lange theory of emotions.

William James [1842–1910] and Carl Lange [1834–1900] posited that a stimulus (such as music) triggers activity in the autonomic nervous system, thereby producing an emotional experience in the brain (Schacter, Gilbert, & Wegner, 2009). In other words, music has a physiological effect before an emotion begins to form or be evidenced.

As a musician creates a sound vocally or instrumentally, it is possible to shape, create, or determine (to some degree) the nature of the intended emotional experience. There can be conscious or unconscious emotional regulation by anyone hearing the musical stimulus, using thought and behavioral strategies to influence the emotion that is consciously or unconsciously recognized as an emerging sensation. Neural arousal leads to an individually determined response (reappraisal of the meaning of the sound) that changes the meaning of the emotion-eliciting stimulus (a valence for or toward the feeling due to the music).

Therefore, the emotion evoked by a particular bit of music may not have a universal effect, but due to both nature and nurture, the listener imputes a chosen emotion. For example, if the listener has read that the music of Gustav Mahler [1860–1911] is somber, the listener may perceive a Mahler composition accordingly. There is, to some extent, a "preordained outcome."

The social perspective set forth in this book emphasizes, among other things, the interactive influence between the musical self-concept and social relations. By experiencing music, whether as a musician or listener, the person is establishing emotional expectations on oneself and others, which involve the reinforcement principle. Recall the example in Chapter Seven in which a wife said, "I want my husband to practice each day because it wards off grumpiness." Or think about how a performer or conductor talks to the audience, commonly in a jovial way, attempting to prime the listeners for a positive response. And then there are the music educators who use music to increase motivation for learning and positivism toward being in school.

An emotionalized musical expectation leads to responses. such as communications or actions between people, that create so-called "social emergence"; that is, socialization becomes an important motivation. Denora (2010) delves into the affective character of identification with social exchanges (the emotion inherent to interpersonal interactions), which would potentially include the music-social interface, and states: "Current work on music as a dynamic medium in social life has highlighted music's role as providing a structure or container for feeling, one whose specific properties contribute to the shape and quality of feeling as it is articulated and sustained within and between individuals as part of the fabrication of ongoing social existence. In short, music offers a resource for the practical constitution of entities we know as 'selves' and also for states we refer to as 'intersubjective'" (p. 178).

Comprehensive Musicianship

Moving into comprehensive musicianship, it is fitting and proper to underscore that emotion-based motivations, stimuli, intentions, expectations, and interpretations are interwoven into every contextual musical-social exchange (again, such as communications or actions) between musician and listener.

As stated at the outset of this chapter, I wish to offer guidance for unifying the seven sectors of musicianship—listening, learning (including analysis of musical elements), practicing, teaching, arranging, composing, and performing. Obviously the chosen route to comprehensive musicianship must be determined by idiosyncratic or individualized consideration.

As a predicate for exploring comprehensive musicianship, it should be recognized that the search for musicianship is never completed fully (I will discuss this issue more later). Thus, the question about whether comprehensive musicianship is determined by achieving (or at least seeking) excellence in all seven sectors of musicianship or sensing fulfillment from accomplishments in just some of the sectors pretty much answers itself. There can never be fully complete musicianship. But there should be a commitment to move toward excellence in potentially all seven sectors of musicianship.

Informal versus Formal Musicianship

There may have been a time when a commercial musician (one who seeks financial compensation or is employed as a performer) could be a successful vocalist on the strength of his or her voice quality or an instrumentalist simply by technical mastery of the instrument. In point of fact, musical competency acquired by informal (vernacular) efforts was never the optimum. It should be noted that vernacular refers to efforts in everyday life (Cohen, 2006); although formal learning with an instructor is not necessary, the vernacular musician may, of course, engage in self-directed learning.

Comprehensive musicianship embraces being competent to understand, appreciate, and (for some people) teach, compose, arrange, and perform outside of a single (or limited number of) musical genre(s). For comprehensive musicianship, embracing multiple musical genres is a prerequisite issue and ideal.

Despite his success as a cornetist, pianist, and composer, Bix Beiderbeck always regretted that he could not read music! Granted, he had an outstanding "ear" and peerless jazz creativity, but he was well aware that he was, as he said, a "musical degenerate." He recognized that a theoretical background would have been an asset and allowed him to improve upon and maximize his creativity. He referred to those with a formal music education as "confirmed musicians" (Lion, 2007, see p. 164).

Using Beiderbeck's term, being a confirmed musician is essential to comprehensive musicianship. Although a performer like Bix Beiderbeck may gain celebrity, there are many musicians who, because of their formal musical training and artistic experiences, unquestionably surpass certain musical celebrities. The point is simple: celebrity is not an essential ingredient of comprehensive musicianship.

As another example of how formal knowledge would have improved musicianship, a mislabeled "master class" was being "taught" by a celebrity instrumentalist. Rightly or wrongly, his approach to teaching was to play the passages, but he had difficulty explaining the inherent musical elements. After playing one passage several times (with great technical flare), one of the students asked, "What is that note that you ended up on each time?" The performer looked somewhat abashed, and confessed, "I'm sorry, I don't know the names of the notes." In contrast, in a master class taught by Wynton Marsalis [1961-   ], his astute explanation of musical elements in passages that he played or sang gave witness to his formal knowledge of music. Incidentally, the fact that Mr. Marsalis embraces numerous genres, various styles, and different types of ensembles, and teaches, arranges, composes, etc., seems to justify that he is a prototype for moving towards comprehensive musicianship.

Individualizing Musicianship

Comprehensive musicianship requires individuation. Neither musician nor listener should think that the qualities of a given musician should follow or be determined by those of another or a conjured up ideal musician.

Perhaps as a way of avoiding the mandatory knuckling down and learning music (including analysis of the musical elements), some would-be musicians tend to engage in considerable imitation of particular musicians. For example, they may harbor self-serving beliefs aligned with celebrity performers ("I just want to sing that tune note for note like Ella Fitzgerald"), which of course may not be accurate ("Bird never practiced for hours"). There is disregard for individual differences, often neglecting the fact that formal study of music can cultivate unique qualities.

For example, there is a common stereotype that Nashville musicians who play country music are unschooled or naïve about music theory. On the contrary, I have found that (not surprisingly, given the realities of being commercially successful) that a goodly number of these musicians hold advanced degrees in music and are not lacking knowledge of musical theory, composition, history, or whatever (for example, see Woody, 2009a). Indeed, in addition to their work within the country genre, a number of these musicians perform with classical, jazz, rock, and popular ensembles. Several of my Nashville acquaintances tour with country music notables, and play as well with major symphonies.

Recall what has been said about how stringent alignment with one (or a few) musical genre(s) reflects poorly on the musician's or listener's musicality. Not only does such exclusiveness lessen musicianship, it can decrease the quality of the social relations that would potentially benefit listening, learning (including analysis of musical elements), practicing, teaching, arranging, composing, and performing music. Capitalizing on one's unique individual talent and ability is part of the search for comprehensive musicianship.

Musical Abilities

The search for comprehensive musicianship also requires maximizing musical abilities. As mentioned earlier, people vary in their potential musical abilities, in part due to genetics, but the potential can be achieved through motivation, learning, and reinforcement (including through social relations).

According to Gardner (1983. 1993, 1997) and Goleman (2005), the modern notions about multiple intelligences and emotional intelligence support that there is sector for music. Again accepting both nature and nurture, musical ability is: "the ability used to write, recall, play, and understand music. It is clear that musical ability involves multiple subabilities that may be relatively distinct from one another" (VandenBos, 2007, p. 603).

Some children are more endowed for musical potential than other kids, but this does not negate the view that everyone has some degree of musicality. However, as mentioned, developing one's musical potential requires nurture and commitment. North and Hargreaves (2008) adopt a developmental approach, with considerable emphasis on biology and cognition; musical identities "have their origins in biological predispositions towards musicality, and . . . are subsequently shaped by other people, groups, situations, and social institutions that they encounter as they develop in a particular culture" (p. 337). Although their pinpointing of "biological predispositions towards musicality" goes beyond my interpretation of the research (do they weight biological predispositions too heavily?), their research-based conclusions buttress the views expressed throughout this book. The bottom line remains: comprehensive musicianship necessitates maximizing potential musical abilities.

Body-Mind Musicianship

It is a simple truth: The search for complete musicianship supports maximizing physical health. The "King of Jazz," Paul Whiteman [1890–1967], found that maintaining a large orchestra (at times, over twenty, thirty, even up to forty musicians) involved cultivating the human resources. Noting that stamina and hard work are necessary for all musicians, Whiteman is quoted as saying, "Jazz musicianship requires not only talented men; it requires physically fit men" (Rayno, 2003, p. 176).

Because of the integral involvement of the self-concept, the vicissitudes of musicianship (e.g., the uncertainty and stress associated with musical performance) health is an important ingredient of comprehensive musicianship. The long-standing connection between mind and body includes the well-documented vulnerability to so-called "psychosomatic disorders" or health-related limitations, illnesses, and disabilities (such as gastrointestinal problems, fine muscle fatigue, headaches, eye strain, etc.) (Woody, 1980). For example, my playing tennis daily and string bass nightly for quite awhile led to elbow pain that has existed for decades! Hanser (2010) explores a host of physical risks experienced by musicians; however, she also sees benefits and concludes that psychoneuroimmunology can explain the impact of music and emotion on health: "Engaging with music becomes a form of integrative medicine that benefits the whole person" (p. 873).

Many musicians attribute significant importance to engaging in physical fitness as a way of increasing energy for performance. At a more practical level, there is some musical equipment that weighs so much that, without physical strength, the musician would be unable single-handedly to have the essential instrument(s), amplifiers, stands, and so on in place (again, I am speaking from personal experience!).

The search for complete musicianship also supports maximizing mental health. Whenever a group of any kind comes together, it is likely that there will be bona fide mental disorders present in someone. Being a mental health professional, I have noticed severely disturbed people within the ranks of almost every occupation or profession. Although I mentioned early on that being creative or a musician does not have a positive correlation with "neurosis," musicians are not exempt from mental problems.

As the passion for music may co-exist in persons with mental health issues, there can be some unfortunate incidents. Consider the following four examples. One musician insisted on practicing the piano in the wee small hours of the morning, even though this disturbed other tenants in the building; a lawsuit was filed to enjoin the musician. Another (nonprofessional) musician, in order to buy a world-class quality instrument borrowed a very large sum of money, something his family of modest finances could not afford. A penniless young man received a lump sum settlement in a lawsuit, and before the day was over, he had spent the entire amount on musical equipment, even though he did not know how to play any instrument. Tragically, a man used two of his instruments to bludgeon his wife to death (without making light of the situation, one must wonder what had happened in the marriage to lead him to select musical instruments as lethal weapons). Regrettably, all of the foregoing examples are true, and have, in fact, been repeated in similar forms other times.

It may be that amateur musical groups are more prone to mental disturbance than professional groups. The latter are typically stable enough to provide the livelihood for the performers, and any comments or behavior that disrupts their commercial activity, including problematic social relations between personnel, could lead to complaints, followed perhaps by discipline and expulsion. In an amateur steel drum group, disputes over leadership led to dropouts, lessening the ensemble's talent considerably.

Interpersonal Relations

This book has emphasized how social relations impact on musicianship and vice versa. The search for complete musicianship is enhanced by constructive, positive, reinforcing, and enjoyable relationships.

Criticisms, abusive comments, unkind humor, put-downs, pranks or practical jokes, and bossiness may reflect a character or personality disorder (the former term tends to be used by psychoanalytically oriented professionals, whereas the latter term is more eclectic). Such personal characteristics will likely define, restrict, and disrupt social relations and musicianship in an adverse manner. As mentioned earlier, numerous examples show how these disorders connect and lead to or derive from a faulty self-concept. In turn, the faulty self-concept limits positive interpersonal relations.

Especially problematic for interpersonal exchanges is a personality tendency that involves narcissism (having excessive self-concern and over-evaluation of importance), which is due to gross personal insecurity. For example, maladaptive behaviors may reflect emotional instability, and deficits in emotional regulation (Gunderson, 2001; Nolen-Hoeksema, 2011). Emotional regulation may be physiologically based (Linehan, Cochran, & Kehrer, 2001).

Although seeming inane, "cultural snobbery" among musicians, much like "disciplinary snobbery" among health care professionals, is a reflection of significant personal insecurity and faulty self-concept. Comments that denigrate a certain kind of music or any musician reflect negatively on the personal qualities and musical self-concept of the castigator.

The concept of complete musicianship does not countenance any semblance of narcissism or other adverse character or personality disorders. Since positive interpersonal relations are essential to moving towards complete musicianship, it is important to be aware and counteract intrapersonal qualities that might jeopardize establishing healthy social relations.

Creative Improvisation

There are four types of instrumentalists: readers, fakers, historians, and masters (of course, with each type, there may be individual differences to some extent, perhaps with a musician being aligned with one or more secondary categories). Readers rely totally on a printed score. Fakers are unable to read music but can play with (perhaps) respectable quality by "ear." Historians have a keen ability for memorization of printed scores and music that has been heard, but do not go into variations or improvisation. Masters can do all that is done by readers, fakers, and historians, but go even further. For musicianship, the master embraces constantly striving for advancement in musical ability, artistic expression, and creativity.

Complete musicianship is an ideal that supports a quest for master status. There can be no rationalizations; there must be consistent commitment to moving towards musical excellence. However, just as Abraham Maslow [1908–1970] (1962) indicated that self-actualization (the fulfillment of potential for the self-concept) was unachievable—there is always the possibility of additional psychological growth—total mastery for musicianship is an impossible (but honorable) dream.

Perhaps the distinguishing quality of the master musician is the ability to improvise. For centuries, improvisation has been inherent to classical music, such as by Bach and Mozart (Walton, 1972). As American jazz evolved, improvisation became a defining characteristic (Tirro, 1977). Various cultural contexts have relied on improvisation in vocal music (Walton, 1972).

When improvising in a performance, a musician should be able to "build a coherent story, to follow a logical development . . . creating emotion, giving up all artificial and sensational effects" (Lion, 2007, p. 64). There is a need for a range of emotion, tenderness, and passion.

From a psychological perspective, any attempt to discount or avoid improvisation based on the history or current status of any musical genre or any particular instrument might be explained as an illogical attempt to establish an ego defense. Stated differently, closed-mindedness about improvisation comes from within the mind of the performer, not from musicianship.

Regrettably, human nature, even at the master stage, tends to lead to routine or habit. For example, a commercial musician playing the same tunes frequently is subject to repeating similar (even the same) "improvisations" (Tirro, 1977). Within commercial music in any genre, there is the possibility that, to please the audience, the musicians will produce essentially the same improvised sounds, avoiding experimentation (Menius, 1999). Believing that avoiding exertion justifies reproduction of the same melodies, variations, or harmonies reflects a lessening of psychological motivation for achieving optimum musicianship.

Interestingly, comprehensive musicianship includes knowledge of music theory, but over analyzing music can be a detriment to improvisation (Tuttle, 1999). Jazz violinist Jean-Luc Ponty [1942–   ] has indicated that he avoids analysis and clichés (established patterns): "Otherwise I let myself be taken by the feeling of a particular piece and try to improvise with emotion. I'm going more for the emotional aspect than thinking what notes I can play. Except that when it is intricate chord changes or rhythms, I practice my solos in advance. I just become familiar with them by playing them over and over at home, so that once I am on stage, I try to come up with new ideas but I know the frame, I know what feeds on those chord changes" (Anick, 1998/1999, p. 14)

Psychologically, being fixated or obsessed with musical structure (i.e., over analysis) places the performer in a musical straitjacket, one that will not allow the release of creativity. For optimal improvisation, the mind of the musician should, although retaining conscious knowledge of the musical structure and elements, promote experimentation and innovation—and the intended musical message.

Improvisation is intended to create and convey a musical message. A key indicator of novice improvisation is evident when the musician plays a lot of notes, often in scales or arpeggios, that offer no musical message. The melody should not be short-changed. Unless a particular stylistic improvisation is desired, the melody should move into an equally lyrical improvisation (Tuttle, 1999). The musician should, in a metaphorical sense, use the voice or instrument to "sing" a lyrical message.

Selecting from the menu of musical elements cannot, of course, be a hodgepodge or potpourri of meaningless sounds; it must represent a musical message. The musical elements that are incorporated into improvisation cannot be a crude amalgamation of bits and pieces. There must be a meaningful integration.

No doubt there is a distinct self-concept quality (e.g., sense of self worth or esteem) necessary to maximize musical expression. Achieving an impressive lyrical quality necessitates personal characteristics that contribute emotional meaning to the music.

Improvisation is dependent upon the personal attributes of the performer, and is a product of knowledge and understanding of music theory and technical mastery of the instrument. If the musician does not studiously pursue and acquire technical skills, as well as musical comprehension, creative improvisation may never be possible. Technical skills and musical comprehension connect to being able to craft a performance. Therefore, the principle is: The beginning musician should walk before running, that is, obtain technical skills and musical comprehension before attempting to improvise.

CODA

If the musical self-concept is the ultimate determinant of comprehensive musicianship and the concomitant social relations, then improvisation is the penultimate. The rationale is simple.

For musicianship, improvisation: (1) relies on nature and nurture (neurology, learning); (2) occurs in a social context laced with attributions, beliefs, values, and reinforcements; (3) must be prefaced by musical ability (knowledge of theory, cultivation of skills); (4) is psychologically motivated by an intention to convey a musical message (usually emotional to some extent) to self and/or others (social communication); (5) depends on an array of resources (biological, emotional, financial, social) and opportunities; and (6) reflects idiosyncratic creativity. Since social psychology pertains to human relationships, it seems clear that musicianship injects personal psychological principles into the interpersonal relations and social situations.

Personal qualities, both positive and negative, influence the manifestation of musicianship. If problematic mental features (such as psychopathology, personality disorders, low emotional intelligence) plague the musician, the musical substance will lessen and deteriorate. However, if the musical self-concept is kept on a positive route, musical elements can develop and flourish as much as the individual's resources and opportunities allow.

The musical self-concept depends on efforts to be a fully functioning human being (Maslow, 1968). Although accepting Maslow's framework,

Julius Seeman [1915–2010] (2008) preferred the term "psychologically inte-grated person," which seems to fit well with the musical self-concept. Certainly within musicianship, there should be a core sense of liking, respect, and trust; there should be no unnecessary screening, deflection, or distortion relevant to the existential nature of music. Using data from real-ity (not fantasy) for psychological nourishment, an integrated musician displays flexibility and productivity, self trust and confidence, an internal locus of control (self-responsibility), and maintenance of an open and uncluttered communication system. Much like Maslow's views about self-actualization, Seeman opines that "no one person owns all of these attributes" and "these characteristics are in their total scope nothing less than the celebration of human potentialities" (p. 269).

Is not the preceding sentence the proclamation for the ideal of com-plete musicianship? By appreciating, creating, communicating, hearing, and experiencing music, there is a celebration of human potential and all social relations are enriched.

REFERENCES

Alter, J. B. (1989). Creativity profile of university and conservatory music students. *Creativity Research Journal, 2,* 184–195.

Anick, P. (1998/1999). Jean-Luc Ponty: Exploring the frontiers of jazz violin. *Fiddler Magazine, 5* (4), 9–10 & 12–14.

Aronson, E., Wilson, T. D., & Akert, R. M. (2010). *Social Psychology* (7th ed.). Upper Saddle River, NJ: Prentice-Hall (Pearson Education).

Ball, P. (2010). *The music instinct: How music works and why we can't do without it.* New York: Oxford University Press.

Bamberger, J. (1982). Growing up prodigies: The mid-life crisis. *New Directions for Child Development, 17,* 61–78.

Baumeister, R. F., & Bushman, B. J. (2011). *Social psychology and human nature* (2nd ed.). Belmont, CA: Wadsworth (Cengage Learning).

Baumeister, R. F., Heatherton, T. F., & Tice, D. M. (1994). *Losing control: How and why people fail at self-regulation.* San Diego: Academic Press.

Benjamin, L. T., Jr. (2007). *A brief history of modern psychology.* Malden, MA: Blackwell.

Blacking, J. (1987). *A commonsense view of all music.* Cambridge: Cambridge University Press.

Bloom, A. (1987). *The closing of the American mind.* New York: Simon & Schuster.

Blum, D. (2002). *Love at Goon Park: Harry Harlow and the science of affection.* Cambridge, MA: Perseus.

Brown, J. D. (2006). *Social psychology*. Boston: McGraw-Hill.

Byrd, J. (2003). *It was a trip: On wings of music*. Anaheim Hills, CA: Centerstream.

Campbell, D., & Doman, A. (2011). *Healing at the speed of sound*. New York: Hudson Street.

Chance, P. L., & Chance, E. W. (2002). *Introduction to educational leadership & organizational behavior: Theory to practice*. Larchmont, NY: Eye on Education.

Cohen, R. D. (2006). *Folk music: The basics*. New York: Routledge (Taylor & Francis).

Crawford, H. J., & Strapp, C. M. (1994). Effects of vocal and instrumental music on visuospatial and verbal performance as moderated by studying preference and personality. *Personality and Individual Differences, 16,* 237–245.

Daoussis, L., & McKelvie, S. J. (1986). Musical preferences and effects of music on a reading comprehension test for extraverts and introverts. *Perceptual and Motor Skills, 62,* 283–289.

Darwin, C. (2004). *The descent of man*. J. Moore & A. Desmond (Eds.). London: Penguin.

Denora, T. (2010). Emotion as social emergence: Perspectives from music sociology. In P. N. Juslin & J. A. Sloboda (Eds.), *Handbook of music and emotion: Theory, research, applications* (pp. 159–183). New York: Oxford University Press.

Diamond Rio & Roland, T. (2009). *Beautiful mess*. Nashville, TN: Thomas Nelson.

Dodds, E. R. (1951). *The Greeks and the irrational*. Berkeley: University of California Press.

Eysenck, H. J. (1990). Biological dimensions of personality. In L. A. Pervin (Ed.), *Handbook of personality theory and research* (pp. 244–276). New York: Guilford.

Feingold, A. (1992). Good-looking people are not what we think. *Psychological Bulletin, 111,* 304–341.

Fiske, S. T. (2004). *Social beings: Core motives in social psychology.* Hoboken, NJ: John Wiley.

Franzoi, S. L. (2009). *Social psychology* (5th ed.). Boston: McGraw-Hill.

Freud, S. (1963). Introductory lectures on psycho-analysis. In J. Strachey (Ed. & Trans.), *The standard edition of the complete works of Sigmund Freud* (16, 431–463). London: Hogarth (Original work published in 1937).

Gardner, H. (1983). *Frames of mind: Theory of multiple intelligence.* New York: Basic Books.

Gardner, H. (1993). *Multiple intelligence: The theory of practice.* New York: Basic Books.

Gardner, H. (1997). *Extraordinary minds.* New York: Basic Books.

Gedo, J. E. (1989). *Portraits of the artist.* Hillside, NJ: Analytic Press,

Goleman, D. (1995). *Emotional intelligence.* New York: Bantam.

Goodwin, C. (1986). Audience diversity, participation and interpretation. *Text, 6*(3), 283–316.

Gunderson, J. G. (2001). *Borderline personality disorder: A clinical guide.* Washington, DC: American Psychiatric Publishing.

Hanser, S. B. (2010). Music, health, and well-being. In P. N. Juslin & J. A. Sloboda (Eds.), *Handbook of music and emotion: Theory, research, applications* (pp. 849–877). New York: Oxford University Press.

Harris, J. R. (1998). *The nurture assumption.* New York: Free Press (Simon & Shuster).

Horowitz, A. C., & Bekoff, M. (2007). Naturalizing anthropomorphism: Behavioral prompts to our humanizing animals. *Anthrozoö, 20*(1), 23–35

Johnson, C. E. (2009). *Meeting the ethical challenges of leadership: Casting light or shadow* (3rd ed.). Thousand Oaks, CA: Sage.

Kaufman, L., & Rawlings, D. (2004). The role of personality and musical experiences in shaping music students' intention to become performers. Conference proceedings (August 3–7) from the 8th biennial International Conference of Music Perception and Cognition, Chicago, IL.

Kemp, A. E. (1991). *The musical temperament*. Oxford: Oxford University Press.

Kinsey, A. C., Pomeroy, W. B., Martin, C. E., & Gebhard, P. H. (1953). *Sexual behavior in the human female*. Philadelphia: W. B. Saunders.

Kirnarskaya, D. (2009). *The natural musician: On abilities, giftedness and talent*. (Initially published by Creativity XXI, 2004, translation by M. H. Teeter). New York: Oxford University Press.

LaVoie, J. C., & Collins, B. R. (1975). Effect of youth culture music on high school students' academic performance. *Journal of Youth and Adolescence, 4*, 57–65.

Lehmann, A. C., Sloboda, J A., & Woody, R. H., III. (2007). *Psychology for musicians: Understanding and acquiring the skills*. New York: Oxford University Press.

Levitin, D. J. (2006). *This is your brain on music: The science of a human obsession*. New York: Plume (Penguin).

Linehan, M. M., Cochran, B. N., & Kehrer, C. A. (2001). Dialectic behavior therapy for borderline personality disorder. In D. H. Barlow (Ed.), *Clinical handbook of psychological disorders: A step-by-step treatment manual* (pp. 470–62). New York: Guilford.

Lion, J. P. (2007). *Bix: The definitive biography of a jazz legend*. New York: Continuum International.

Mannes, E. (2011). *The power of music*. New York: Walker.

Maslow, A. (1968). *Toward a psychology of being* (2nd ed.). New York: Van Nostrand Reinhold.

McClelland, D. C., Atkinson, J. W., Clark, R. A., & Lowell, E. L. (1953). *The achievement motive*. New York: Appleton-Century-Crofts.

Menius, A. (1999). The natural thing to do: The Doobie Shea Records story so far. *Bluegrass Unlimited, 33*(7), 42–48.

Myers, D. G. (2008). *Social psychology* (9th ed.). New York: McGraw-Hill.

Nash, A. (2010). *Baby, let's play house*. New York: HarperCollins.

Nietzsche, F. (1974). *The gay science*. Translated by W. Kaufmann. New York: Vintage Books.

Nolen-Hoeksema, S. (2011). *Abnormal psychology* (5th ed.). New York: McGraw-Hill.

North, A. C., & Hargreaves, D. J. (2008). *The social and applied psychology of music.* New York: Oxford University Press.

Northouse, P. G. (2007). *Leadership: Theory and practice* (4th ed.). Thousand Oaks, CA: Sage.

Palmer, B. (2006). A key factor in the sound of a banjo and how you may be able to acquire it more quickly. *The Evolution of the Tone Bell Tone Ring System,* http://www.banjowizard.com/tonebell.htm.

Pavitra, K. S., Chandrashekar, C. R., & Choudhury, P. (2007), Creativity and mental health: A profile of writers and musicians. *Indian Journal of Psychiatry, 49,* 34–43.

Rauscher, F. H. (1997). A cognitive basis for the facilitation of spatial-temporal cognition through music instruction. In V. Brummett (Ed.), *Ithaca conference: 96 music as intelligence: A sourcebook* (pp. 31–44). Ithaca, NY: Ithaca College.

Rauscher, F. H., Shaw, G. L., Levine, L. J., Wright, E. L., Dennis, W. R., & Newcomb, R. L. (1997). Music training causes long-term enhancement of preschool children's spatial-temporal reasoning. *Neurological Research, 19,* 2–8.

Rayno, D. (2003). *Paul Whiteman, Pioneer in American music, Volume I: 1890–1930.* Latham, NJ: Scarecrow Press.

Reid, H., & Reid, D. (2007). *The Statler Brothers.* Nashville, TN: Yell.

Rippere, V. (1977). What's the thing to do when you're feeling depressed? A pilot study. *Behavior Research and Therapy, 15,* 185–191.

Rokeach, M. (1960). *The open and closed mind.* New York: Basic Books.

Rokeach, A. M. (1973). *The nature of human values.* New York: Free Press.

Schacter, D. L., Gilbert, D. T., & Wegner, D. M. (2009). *Psychology.* New York: Worth.

Seeman, J. (2008). *Psychotherapy and the fully functioning person.* Bloomington, IN: AuthorHouse.

Sergent, D., & Thatcher, G. (1974). Intelligence, social status, and musical abilities. *Experimental Research in the Psychology of Music, 2*(2), 52–57.

Shiraev, E. (2011). *A history of psychology: A global perspective.* Thousand Oaks, CA: Sage.

Simonton, D. K. (1999). Talent and its development: An emergenic and epigenetic model. *Psychological Review, 106,* 435–457.

Simonton, D. K. (2000). Creative development as acquired expertise: Theoretical issues and an empirical test. *Developmental Review, 20,* 283–318.

Sloboda, J. A. (1985). *The musical mind.* Oxford: Clarendon.

Sluming, V. A., & Manning, J. T. (2000). Second to fourth digit ratio in elite musicians: Evidence for musical ability as an honest signal of male fitness. *Evolution and Human Behavior, 21,* 1–9.

Sternberg, R. J. (1983). How much gall is too much gall? Review of *Frames of mind: The theory of multiple intelligences. Contemporary Education Review, 2(3),* 215–224.

Storr, A. (1992). *Music and the mind.* New York: Ballantine.

Storr, A. (1993). *The dynamics of creation.* New York: Random House.

Surtees, P. G., Wainwright, N. W. J., Luben, R., Wareham, N. J., Bingham, S. A., & Khaw, K. (2010). Mastery is associated with cardiovascular disease mortality in men and women at apparently low risk. *Health Psychology, 29(4),* 412–420.

Thorndike, E. L. (1905). *The elements of psychology.* New York: A. G. Seiler.

Tirro, F. (1977). *Jazz: A history.* New York: W. W. Norton.

Traub, J. (1998, October 26). Multiple intelligence disorder. *New Republic.*

Tuttle, J. (1999). Darol Anger: Renaissance man of the fiddle. *Fiddler Magazine, 6* (1), 20–25.

VandenBos, G. R. (Ed.). *APA dictionary of psychology.* Washington, DC: American Psychological Association.

Walton, O. M. (1972). *Music: Black, white & blue.* New York: William Morrow.

Woody, R. H. (1978a). Gibson's Julius Bellson: Insights from forty years of experience. *Guitar Player, 12* (3), 30 & 100–101 & 106–107

Woody, R. H. (1978b). Julius Bellson: Master of fretted instruments. *Nebraska Music Educator, 36* (2), 4–5.

Woody, R. H. (1978c). The arts in general education: The professional identity. *Music Educators Journal, 64*(9), 54.

Woody, R. H. (1980). *Bodymind liberation: Achieving holistic health.* Springfield, IL: Thomas.

Woody, R. H. (1981). Wilbur Marker: A view from the inside: 40 years at Gibson. *Guitar Player, 15* (3), 26–28 &30.

Woody, R. H. (1984). *Practical mental health.* Springfield, IL: Thomas.

Woody, R. H. (1999a). Kalamazoo's gentle music professor. *Michigan History, 83*(1), 44–47.

Woody, R. H. (1999b). The musician's personality. *Creativity Research Journal, 12*(4), 241–250.

Woody, R. H. (2009a). Kenny Sears: Premier fiddler on the Grand Ole Opry. *Fiddler Magazine, 16*(Summer, 2), 15–19.

Woody, R. H. (2009b). The psychology of jump-start learning. *American String Teacher, 59*(3), 34–37.

Woody, R. H. (2010). String players' guide to guitar accompaniment. *American String Teacher, 60*(4), 46–47.

Wooten, V. L. (2006). *The music lesson.* New York: Penguin,

Worringer, W. (1963). *Abstraction and empathy.* Translated by M. Bullock. London: Routledge & Kegan Paul.

ABOUT THE AUTHOR

Robert Henley Woody, Sr., is a professor of psychology, an attorney, a psychologist, and a health scientist. Foremost, he considers himself to be a musician.

Dr. Woody has performed on numerous recordings and television and radio programs. After being "on the road," teaching school music, and playing in a myriad of dancehalls and honky-tonks, he turned his interests and talents to higher education.

From Western Michigan University, he holds Bachelor of Music Education (BMus) degree, with performance areas in voice, trumpet, and string bass. He has earned a Master of Arts (MA) and Doctor of Philosophy (PhD) degrees from Michigan State University, Specialist in Education (EdS) degree from Western Michigan University, Doctor of Science (ScD) degree from the University of Pittsburgh (ScD), and law (JD) degree from Creighton University. He has also studied at the Guildhall School of Music and Drama (trumpet with Horace Barker) and Vanderbilt-Blair School of Music (mandolin with Jerome "Butch" Baldassari, and tuba with Gil Long). He has authored numerous scholarly articles and books on education, mental health, law, and musicianship.

After being on the faculties at the State University of New York at Buffalo, the University of Maryland, the Grand Valley State University, and the Ohio University, Dr. Woody became Professor of Psychology (and former Dean for Graduate Studies and Research) at the University of Nebraska at Omaha. He is an active music performer.